HIGH
and
DESPERATE
PLACE

AARDVARK
PRESS

In a HIGH *and* DESPERATE PLACE

Rachel Kelsey Colenso

Foreword by Stephen Venables

AARDVARK
PRESS

© text Rachel Kelsey Colenso 2008
www.kelseyadventures.co.uk
© design and layout Aardvark Press 2008

Aardvark Press Publishing (Pty) Ltd
PO Box 37571, Valyland 7978, Cape Town, South Africa

www.aardvarkpress.co.za

This book was printed in South Africa,
on paper that was produced from managed forests.

ISBN 978-1-920154-04-2

Edited by Dulcie Kirby and Gail Jennings
Design and setting by Ed-venture (www.ed-venture.co.za)

www.kelseycolenso.com

Front cover images:
Rachel Kelsey Colenso © James Calder
Piz Badile © Bruce Goodlad, mountain guide 2008; www.
mountainadventurecompany.com
Cover design by Ed-venture
Printed by Interpak, 22 Willowton Road, Pietermaritzburg

Dedication and thanks

This book is dedicated to Rosemary Acacia Colenso, born 4 July 2007 My daughter, when you read this may you know that God's grace and His power lives through the work of many who serve Him.

My grateful thanks to the Swiss Air Rescue team, Rega, who work long hours and brave dangerous conditions to save the lives of so many people – during the many months spent writing this book I've considered the impact that such people make on the live of others, and how my life has been transformed in so many ways; to my husband, parents and family who have supported my writing; to our friends Avery Cunlithe, Ruth Woolven, Tim Costello and Phil Ashby.

In memory of Richard Hamilton and Seba Canelletti.

Contents

Foreword

I first met Rachel Kelsey on a September morning on the Eiger in 2006. Or at least I saw her and her husband, Jeremy Colenso, in the grey light of dawn edging around a terrifying traverse, heading for a difficult modern rock climb, while we continued up the easier West Flank of the mountain. The actual meeting proper happened a few weeks later at the Alpine Club in London. We quickly found connections which, in this case, went beyond that chance crossing of paths on the Eiger. In particular, I was excited to hear about our many mutual friends in South Africa – a country with some of the finest rock climbing in the world.

Now, reading Rachel's extraordinary book, I discover many more connected threads of experience. The story opens with the frightening events on the flight after Rachel's first ascent of the Spitzkoppe – a unique granite mountain in the Namib desert, which I have also been lucky enough to climb. But the real action – the heart of the story – takes place on another instantly recognisable granite mountain called the Piz Badile, which towers over what is perhaps the most beautiful valley in Switzerland – the Val Bondasca. Rachel's account brought back fond memories of my own visit to that valley, over thirty years ago, and in particular the classic North Ridge of the Piz Badile.

It also brought back the terror of the cataclysmic electric storms for which this region, the Bregaglia, is so notorious. It was during one of those terrible storms that Mario Molteni and Giuseppe Valsecchi died of hypothermia, after completing the first ascent of the Piz Badile's Northeast Face in 1937. And it was a similar storm which struck Rachel and Jeremy on the North Ridge.

I remember well how awkward that ridge is to descend. Every abseil threatens to leave you swinging perilously over the abyss either side of the crest. Even on a fine sunny morning we found it laborious, at times alarming, in a full-blown storm, blasted by lightning then frozen to the core by driving hail and snow – as Rachel and Jeremy were in 2003. It must have been terrifying.

Rachel's courage shines through her fear. It highlights her refusal to give in to weakness, and her determination not to retreat into a solipsistic shell, but to continue working *together*, minute after minute, hour after hour, clinging to hope, nurturing creatively every tiny possibility to live.

This is a universal epic of survival, but it is also a story peculiarly of our times, because escape comes, eventually, as the result of a text message beamed from the storm-lashed alpine ledge to a friend in London. I remember catching the story at the time in a newspaper, and noticing the name of the friend – Avery Cunlithe – a photographer who had recently taken pictures of my son and me. More connections. Now, reading the full story for the first time, I realise just how brilliantly Avery helped sustain the flicker of life from his flat in London, while one of Switzerland's magnificent helicopter rescue teams did the same closer to the mountain, pushing their own skills to the limit in atrocious flying conditions. Having myself once been rescued – in my case by equally brave Indian pilots – I can identify with that lump-in-the-throat surge of emotion at the moment of rescue, and the gratitude at being given another chance at life. In Rachel's case that new life was all the more precious because it was the storm on the Badile which cemented the tentative bond between her and Jeremy Colenso, resulting in their marriage, so that this story of survival is also a most moving love story.

Stephen Venables, May 2008

1   The Piz Badile

In the beginning God created the heavens and the earth.
GENESIS 1:1

The small aeroplane drops from the desert sky. Wind screams over its body as it hurtles toward the red sands where the Kalahari and Namib dunes meet. The only inhabitants of this arid region in western Botswana are small tribes of San Bushmen living in circular *kraals* of huts made from sticks. There is no time to radio for help. It will be days, perhaps weeks before the wreck is discovered. Inside the aircraft are four people, trapped and awaiting their fate. I'm one of the four. We're returning from my first rock climbing expedition, an attempt to climb Spitzkoppe in Namibia. My parents had helped me afford the adventure as a gift for my twenty-first birthday.

My stomach hits the roof of my mouth. It feels like a continual downward swoop on a rollercoaster. The altimeter has dropped from ten thousand feet, nine thousand ... I can't believe this is happening. A scream escapes. My body is disconnected from my brain. Instinctive reactions take over. Next to me in the front seat the pilot pushes his arm across me. He reaches for a small switch on the side panel, the switch to change fuel tanks. We're supposed to have seventy-five minutes' fuel in each of the four tanks, but the journey across the desert from Windhoek in Namibia to Maun in Botswana required us to economise. The recommended switchover time was sixty-eight minutes but, even bleeding the tanks to two minutes short of empty, at seventy-three minutes per tank, we would have had just enough fuel to circle Maun airstrip for fifteen minutes, and no option to land elsewhere. This is probably the first time a Piper Cherokee aircraft has made this journey, and now I understand why.

The engine splutters as fresh fuel feeds it. Our salvation depends on the plane remaining aloft. The engine roars. We look at each other, ashen-faced and relieved.

Again the engine chokes, falters, cuts out. We plummet again. The pilot fights his controls as the craft veers into a nosedive. My heart sinks. At that moment, fuel miraculously surges through the system and the small craft thrusts forward and regains its strength.

❋ ❋ ❋ ❋ ❋

Twelve years on – the anniversary of that epic – and it all seems a world away. It's a hot summer evening in late August 2003. The London climbing centre is crowded and people are bobbing about on the wall like spiders on brightly-coloured webs. It's too busy to train seriously, so I sling my rope over my shoulder and clip my shoes to my harness, ready to leave.

A young man approaches. We start chatting. He has thick, dark hair and deep blue eyes. He is lean, muscular and, at five foot nine, just a touch taller than myself. We had first spoken to each other some ten years before at a climbing competition when we were students in South Africa. More recently we'd met up again and spent a couple of days scaling the coastal cliffs of Devon – and jumping into the sea afterwards. He is slightly hesitant, as if he has something important to say. His studious expression reveals little.

I wait, studying the edging on my climbing shoes so as not appear overly keen. The only men I meet seem to be married, or overweight and overworked. Is he going to ask me on a date? I know better, though, than to think that a date with Jeremy will be dinner and movies.

Jeremy is a rock and alpine climber who has completed many first and technical ascents. He has won various sport climbing competitions and competed in the World Cup in 1993. He must sense my apprehension. His face breaks into a broad grin accentuated by deep smile lines.

This isn't the best time for me to meet a potential date, right after climbing and in need of a shower. I probably look like a scarecrow. I run fingers self-consciously through my long, flaxen strands, hoping to improve the look.

We talk a while, and then he suggests we fly to Venice, Italy.

I try not to look surprised. OK, so we had been for pizza together, shared a drink with a friend, climbed a couple of routes, but ... Venice? Is he serious? I've always fancied the idea of going to Venice, and floating lazily down the canals on a gondola, sipping wine and appreciating the fine Venetian architecture. How romantic! I start going through my wardrobe in my mind. I will need to buy a new dress.

In Venice, he says, we will hire a car and head north. I've never really considered what the north of Italy is like, but guess it must be pretty romantic, too. He mentions driving beside Lake Como. That bit sounds good. Then he speaks of crossing the border into the Swiss Alps, and I start to get the picture.

The European Alps stretch over a vast area. With their jagged forms and deep, glaciated lakes, their magnificent ranges have inspired people for centuries. They extend from the Maritime Alps in the south of France and sweep eastward in a giant arc around the north of the Italian peninsula, and to the Julian Alps in Slovenia a thousand kilometres away. The mountains were formed more than seventy million years ago – a result of pressure from the African landmass as it shifted north. The compressing action created great folds, or *nappes*, that rose out of the sea like dragons, often breaking and sliding one over one another to form gigantic thrust faults.

Much later, glaciation carved out the mountain landscape to create distinctive features such as sharp angled cliffs, or *aiguilles*, that point up to the skies like spearheads. High up the slopes are hidden, carved-out hollows, or *cirques*, with small crystal lakes at their bases. Towering over lesser formations are the twisted and pointed matterhorn peaks and hanging valleys, their beauty reflected in the dappled waters of long moraine-blocked lakes such as Garda, Como, and Geneva in the north.

The alpine geology and weather pose many challenges for those wishing to climb them. I'm beginning to doubt the new dress will be necessary. I'll probably have to spend the money on a decent set of waterproofs instead.

For millennia people have inhabited the valleys, travelled the passes, and explored the lower Alpine slopes. Before 1912 the only access to the high peaks from the valley floor some two thousand metres below, was on foot.

Interest in the 'dramatic, terrifying and awesome' during the nineteenth century led to a growing fascination for mountains among wealthy explorers and academics. Alpine peaks became the new playground for tourists and adventurers. They ventured out with ladders to stretch across crevasses, and from which the brave-hearted could peer into the depths of the icy world below and admire, or become terrified by, the view.

Crystal gatherers moved higher into the mountains in search of stones to sell in the valley markets. In the beginning, a simple *alpenstock*, similar to a shepherd's staff, was all they had to steady their balance on steep-sided mountains. In time, their explorations led them to develop equipment so that they could cross glaciers and reach higher up the snow-covered slopes. The *alpenstock* became the first wooden-shaft ice axe. To prevent their feet from slipping, they attached sharp spikes to the soles of their shoe – the first crampons. Avid mountain explorers made further developments that enabled them to reach the tops of many peaks. A number of mountaineering pioneers immortalised their names by summitting virgin peaks. Later a second generation built upon these advances by making first ascents up more technically difficult faces. Subsequently, a hierarchy of mountaineering achievements developed. Climbs became classified according to their technical difficulty, length, and relative danger.

Within the Alps one group of climbs stands out as the benchmark for extreme mountaineering. These are the six big north faces: the Eiger, the Matterhorn, the Grandes Jorasses, the Cima Grande, the Petite Dru, and the Piz Badile – climbs the esteemed International Mountain Guides Association holds as being the pinnacle of alpine achievement.

Today, just one generation later, with the effects of climate change, they pose an even greater challenge. With large areas of near vertical rock and ice, the north-facing aspect of each of these mountains can become of arctic temperature and completely inhospitable. With changes in climate patterns and generally warmer temperatures in the summer months, the mountain weather cycles have become less predictable, and the geological formations less stable. Permafrost once glued together the loose rubble of these mountains all year round. Now, many of the routes have become too treacherous to climb in all but the most severe of cold winters.

As I drive home I mull over Jeremy's suggestion that we climb the North Face of the Piz Badile.

The Piz Badile is the most famous mountain in the Bregaglia region. It is not the highest, nor does it span the greatest surface area, but it possesses a history marked by triumph and tragedy. For much of the year it's shrouded in cloud and cloaked in ice. At an altitude of 3 308 metres, its southern slopes extend into Italy and its north face is just inside Switzerland.

Piz Badile in Italian means 'shovel'. This describes its shape – and its appearance, too. Like the metal plate of a shovel, its grey face is sheer and slippery. This makes the northern side virtually unclimbable in all but the good weather of late summer or autumn.

Beyond the southern slopes of the mountain, northern Italy is fairly flat, with rolling plains and dryer, arable land. During summer, hot air rises off the plains, forming a localised low-pressure system. This low pressure is then pushed north. The first range of mountains it reaches is the Bregaglia Alps and, within this range, the first mountain it hits is the Piz Badile.

This region, and particularly this mountain, is home to some of the most spectacular electric storms witnessed in the Alps. It may be no coincidence that the scientist Alessandro Volta, who gave his name to the unit of electricity, and who invented the battery in the eighteenth century, was born and grew up in the region fairly close to the Piz Badile.

One of the most famous alpine pioneers, and possibly Italy's most famous alpinist, Riccardo Cassin, first ascended its northern flanks in 1937. He has been awarded four medals for extreme athleticism, and has been designated *Grande Ufficiale della Republica* (Grand Official Representative of the Republic), in recognition of his remarkable climbing feats. He is either an honorary member or honorary president of National Alpine clubs in Italy, Switzerland, France, Spain, and the USA. Among his many achievements were new routes on the Grandes Jorasses, the Cima Grande and the Piz Badile.

For experienced contemporary alpinists, many of Cassin's first ascents are extreme test pieces. In 1961 Cassin and the famous Spiders of Lecco group, received a telegram offering congratulations from the then-President of the USA, John F Kennedy, after their successful first summit of the south face of the 6 194 metre Mount McKinley (Denali), the highest mountain in North America.

This remarkable alpinist gave a harrowing account of his first ascent of the north-east face of the Piz Badile. He described the face as a "wall of granite, one thousand metres' high, set in severe and gloomy surroundings".

In 1937 Cassin set out with two good friends, Ratti and Esposito, to attempt the great wall. At the base of the wall they came across two men from Como, Molteni and Valsecchi, who had reached the granite face some hours earlier. The five men continued as one team, roped together.

The second day presented technical difficulties, made worse by cascades of stones showering down from above. One such avalanche carried away Molteni's rucksack of provisions, and the team had to share their supplies, including their whisky. Next, they were subjected to a rainstorm. Prolonged exposure to the cold weather weakened Molteni and Valsecchi. Finally, in a state of exhaustion, they summited the mountain in a storm, and began the arduous descent down the Italian side. Poor visibility and diminishing daylight further tested them. First Molteni fell and, although the team tried to help, he was never to rise again. Later the exhausted Valsecchi, dazed by the recent loss of his climbing partner, paused by a boulder where his life slipped from him. The three remaining men staggered back and survived. This was a costly expedition. Nearly half the team who climbed the route had perished. I console myself thinking that history will be unlikely to repeat itself.

Certainly we have advances in equipment technology on our side. Methods of ascent have changed radically since those first Alpine explorers pushed their axes into the steep, snow slopes, carrying heavy ladders with which to span crevasses. At least we won't be lugging huge coils of hawser-laid rope and whole necklaces of steel carabiners up the mountain.

Then there were the hobnailed boots. How awkward it must have been to climb slippery rock faces in such cumbersome footwear. They had teeth attached to them, called 'clinkers' and 'triconies', which were supposed to bite into the rock. I've met climbers who used this old style of climbing boot, and who recount vividly their experiences of edging up vertical rock faces by digging the small metal points into fissures and knobbly protrusions. Today my climbing boots are little leather efforts with sticky rubber soles made from the same substance used for tyres on top racing cars. And they're able to adhere to almost anything, provided it is dry.

Each culture has its own way of approaching climbing, and each favours particular methods of ascent and equipment. On the whole, the French wait for perfect weather and climb their routes quickly, in good style, to get home in time for tea. What is not their style is weighting themselves down carrying cookers and 'bivi' equipment, and which slows everything and inevitably forces one to spend a cold night out huddling on a ledge.

Generally bivi equipment includes sleeping bags or, at the very least a bivi bag each, warm clothing, an extra meal to keep one going, possibly a gas or petrol stove and an aluminium cooking pot in which to melt snow for a warm drink. American Alpinist Yvon Chouinard summed it up by saying: "If you take bivouac equipment along, you will bivouac."

And then there's the queuing. In British climbing, there is an unwritten law to queuing. Climbers uncoil their rope at the bottom of the route. This designates their position in the queue. So as not to intrude, they will then wait until the party ahead has moved sufficiently upwards. On a longer route, if the party ahead is terribly slow, the leader will catch up with the second climber of the slow party and ask if it would be possible to overtake at a suitable stance. If the slower leader is gracious enough – which most often is the case – the faster climbers will be allowed to pass while the slower ones wait until the others are far enough ahead so as not to become tangled in each other's ropes, or to hear each other's conversation. Having now learned the British system I quite like it, except at those times when there are three ropes coiled at the base of the route I've planned to climb.

The Swiss-Italian Bregaglia is quite different. Climbers have, by their own admission, developed a system that is similar to the Italian approach to driving. It's recommended in the modern, local guidebooks that you, "push in and abseil or climb over whomever is in the way ... climb fast and be pushy unless you relish being treated as a moving obstacle."

I'm not really keen to become a moving object. It seals my decision. If we're to attempt this climb, it will be now, outside the European summer vacation time. This way we'll be less likely to encounter another party.

The next day, during a really boring stretch of work, I begin to analyse Jeremy's proposal. Is it feasible? How much do we really know about each other? Shouldn't something as big as this require more thought than merely being impressed by a person's abilities, or by the assumption that we'll get on?

That he's asked me shouldn't come as such a surprise. We'd spoken previously about the area and the route. I guess it just hadn't occurred to me he was considering me as his climbing partner.

The majority of climbers I've met are men. Not all of them immediately take to the idea that a woman has equal experience in such activities. From previous climbs I'd noticed Jeremy's approach is different. He believes a team requires individuals with different strengths and weaknesses, enabling all an active role in the planning and preparation of routes about to be climbed.

Jeremy is a patient, solid and meticulous climber, with an appetite for adventure. On the climbs we'd done he'd valued my knowledge in rope work, navigation and related outdoor expertise.

On the whole I feel we're complementary personalities. If you know yourself, your own strengths and needs, it's easier to recognise the same in others. This allows one to get along well when placed in stressful situations.

My knowledge of how teams operate effectively was enhanced in 2005 when I organised and led an all-women expedition to explore an uncharted region of Guyana in the Amazon. The maps were fifty years out of date, with large empty areas labelled, 'cloud cover'. GPS systems don't work well under the thick tree canopy either. As a result much of the area has remained unexplored.

At the time, the aim of our expedition was to promote eco-tourism to Guyana by creating a trail that others could follow in the future. As part of our sponsorship we were offered psychological support while team-building for the event. Our psychologist, Dr Robert Kovach, believes there are four phases that effective teams undergo in order to succeed: 'forming', 'storming', 'norming' and 'performing'. Many teams get stuck somewhere along the way, and so don't manage to use their team's combined abilities to full potential.

The first stage, 'forming', is when team members meet for the first time and are on their best behaviour. 'Storming' enables people to vent their differences and come up with a new set of conclusions, and a new way of viewing the team and working together. The 'norming' phase is the settling process where, with new insights, the team resolves to work together. The 'performing' stage is when a team is able to use the insight its members have gained to maximise each other's strengths, thereby creating a synergy through gelling cohesively as a team. As such the positive experience of combined success will fuel further successes. Practice not only makes perfect, but also irons out problems. So far, on our climbs and time spent together, Jeremy and I seem to be 'norming'.

2 Hope, fear and ambition

For every minute spent in organising, an hour is earned.
BENJAMIN FRANKLIN

"Hello. What are you up to?"

"Oh hi, is that ... who is it?" I venture, not wanting Jeremy to assume I've been waiting for his call.

"Ye-es." His slow reply confirms he isn't fooled by my hesitation.

We talk a while about the new information – the route, his latest 'weather' searches on the internet and the possibility of our having some of the best weather the region has experienced in a while. Everything will be dry. It might even still be warm enough to climb in short sleeves.

"So, what are you doing on Friday evening?" Jeremy asks. "I thought, if you wanted, I could show you the stuff in this guidebook, and we could have a look at the map?"

I'd planned to meet some friends in Kensington, so I suggest we have a drink beforehand, and that perhaps Jeremy might like to join our group afterwards.

Over the next couple of days I hardly work. I surf the internet searching for more information, checking the weather and, between times, checking my boxes of climbing equipment to make sure everything is still there. Friday rolls on. Soon we're sipping a glass of wine in a restaurant and poring over a topographical map of the Piz Badile.

Although this mountain is not the highest or most difficult in the world, we'll be climbing it alone, without support from a team at base, and without guides. This is the way we've been trained to climb – as self-sufficient parties where all the decision-making and risks are taken solely by us.

I'm keen to find out what sort of timeline Jeremy has in mind. What will the cost be? Do we need to book permits in advance? Where will we leave the hire car? What is the walk-in like? And the descent? Some mountains are difficult to get to, and tricky or dangerous to exit. What will our back-up plan be if we find the route out of condition, or if there is something else unforeseen? It's easy to get wrapped up in the technical part of the climb and so to overlook other important practical aspects.

While big expeditions depend on mules, yaks and sherpas, this type of Alpine route will rely on our own strength and ability. I'm sure I have the skills to do it, but whether I'm fast enough by Jeremy's standards is another thing. Would Jeremy prefer a male companion? Someone physically stronger and faster, someone able to carry heavy loads. The walk-in will take quite a few hours, and will involve lugging bivi and climbing equipment up more than one and a half thousand metres of vertical ascent even before the technical climbing starts.

Most of all I need to know why Jeremy is keen to climb this particular mountain. Sometimes people want to accomplish a challenge at all costs – and sometimes it really is at all costs. I don't wish to become enmeshed in one of those set-ups where human life takes second place to personal achievement.

Jeremy

Summer 2003 was a record season for temperature and dryness. The North Face of the Piz Badile is a rock route flanked by a glacier. With its orientation and angle, the Face can hold snow and water run-off until very late in the summer.

I had walked to the base of the route after my ascent of the Comici Route on the North Face of the Cima Grande, and confirmed that it was indeed in a condition to be climbed. Unfortunately I'd had to return home, but every day I would look at several weather sites on the internet. Over an extended period I was able to determine that the conditions remained largely unchanged. I also spoke to friends who had recently climbed in the general area.

When I'd looked up at the mountain on my reconnaissance, my fingers had itched to climb it. It has one of the most beautiful faces in the Alps. It reminded me of mountains I had climbed as a teenager in the wilderness of the Western Cape, South Africa. In particular, it reminded me of a climbing location called the Yellowwood Amphitheatre in the Du Toit's Kloof Pass. The Piz Badile is in a similarly remote region of the Alps. Both cliffs are perfect geometric shapes on a massive scale, and both have a similar approach through dense indigenous vegetation.

For me the Piz Badile seemed like a challenge that would combine all my years of preparation, skill and experience.

Rachel and I had never climbed together in South Africa, but there was something reassuring about her familiar accent, coupled with the fact that we'd had mutual climbing partners, and had both done climbs in South Africa that are accepted 'rites of passage'.

From seeing her win several national competitions in South Africa, I knew Rachel was a technically proficient climber. These skills were confirmed in the training we did, in particular the sea-cliff climbs. Rachel was able to judge the soundness of fixed protection, to set up safe belays quickly, both on the abseil descents and en route while climbing back out. She wasn't perturbed by variable rock quality and seemed to take it all in her stride. She was exuberant and highly presentable – a refreshing departure from the smelly and stubbly partners I had shared climbing experiences with in the past.

At the time Jeremy mentions the possibility of doing this climb, I'm desperate to get out of London, to be part of nature again. Throughout our upbringing, my brother and I had enjoyed the freedom of roaming wild. Our bond with nature was deepened through our parents taking us on safaris to the most remote regions of southern Africa. Later as students we had maintained our connection with nature through sport. Julian, my brother, had been an avid surfer. For me it was climbing. My first experiences were barefoot – I simply did not have the money to spend on climbing gear, and I didn't expect my parents to provide for this luxury either. Eventually I became accomplished enough to obtain sponsorship and went on to compete internationally in adventure racing.

My ambitions developed into bigger climbing and sports-related expeditions, visiting remote regions of North America, South America and the Himalayas.

My time spent climbing Italian icefalls with a good London-based, American friend called Avery had whet my appetite to explore more of this beautiful country. I can't wait to return to the mountains in Italy. The Piz Badile appeals to my enthusiasm for adventure and to my determination to succeed in a technical challenge.

In theory all I need to do is commit to the idea and to start preparing. It sounds like quite an easy step, but simply saying 'yes' is sometimes difficult.

Jeremy listens to my concerns. We agree on some practice climbs together in north Wales and on Holyhead Island. If the weather in the Alps is still looking good, we can take things further.

Instantly I'm reassured and motivated.

After a few more days of climbing together, I start making lists – lists of what I have, what I need to get and what I'm not sure about. Planning such trips takes a great deal of effort. One learns from experience to make provision for the ten percent of preparations that take ninety percent of the time.

Jeremy and I meet a couple of times to go through our packing. It would be silly for us to replicate items like the First Aid kit, and I'm also keen to know his formula for his most recent success on the Comici Route.

Jeremy shows me the rucksack he used for the climb. It sits on his back like a small jetpack. I can't help but imagine him pulling a release cord and taking off. At first I cannot believe one is able to fit everything into such a tiny bag. I had always used something bigger, but filled only half way. Jeremy insists that all the extreme rock alpinists in France nowadays tend to favour this type of rucksack. His theory is that if you carry a bigger bag, you end up carrying equipment you generally won't need, and which slows you down. I agree, realising how easy it is to throw in extra items, rather than taking the time and effort to meticulously select what you will require.

Our meetings and telephone calls become more and more about our preparations, and less and less about just getting to know each other. We sip coffee whilst poring over Alpine maps. We underline extracts from guidebooks. We practise climbing together and the different tactics needed to make things faster and more efficient.

The route is well within our technical abilities, the hardest pitches certainly a few grades below what Jeremy can comfortably lead ahead on and where I can follow.

We measure our estimated time on routes of varying difficulty. We estimate how long it will take us to set up belays and to swap over lead-climbing positions. We translate this information on to the larger scale of the mountain, taking into consideration fatigue and conditions which may not be perfect, such as wet or icy bits of rock. We allow latitude for route finding, and for unforeseen events such as a rope getting caught on something, or for a section that might recently have changed due to rock fall. Then we estimate it will take us twelve to fourteen hours to complete the climb, perhaps eighteen hours if there is some difficulty along the way. To climb the route in this time we will need to adopt a very fast and light approach. It's now accepted practice to climb this way, at it is ultimately often safer. In the past alpinists armed themselves with cumbersome equipment, dragging it behind them, taking days to accomplish one climb.

I opt to borrow Jeremy's spare, green, mini rucksack. It holds twenty-five litres, and has an elastic mesh on the outside in which to stash chocolate and energy bars. My waterproofs are too big to squash inside. They need replacing. I purchase a tiny, super-light, blue technical mountaineering jacket and black breathable over-trousers. Together they take up just two fistfuls of space. In fact, the thing that seems to take up the most room is a two and a half litre water container and its drinking tube. We also pack a survival shelter which, should we need it, will give us protection against the elements for a few hours.

We decide that we'll walk up to the climb in technical approach shoes. These are designed for scrambling over rocky, alpine terrain and can be squashed into our small day sacks for the climb.

I also remember to wind a little insulation tape around a small pencil. This is good for repairs and will seal my drinking bottle so the tube can't unscrew inside the rucksack and spill over everything – as happened once before.

We consider carefully what food to take with us, whether to take a stove, and where we might be able to stash stoves and sleeping bags.

We pack our lightest carabiners, and our superior technical ropes which handle well in a variety of conditions. We strap small cutting blades to the sides of our helmets, a lighter option than a Swiss army knife. We search for extremely light head torches that can be stored in the side pockets of our jackets, their spare batteries taped to the lid of the First Aid kit. We each take a dustbin liner into which we can put a small fleece and pair of gloves and which can also serve as an emergency dry bag.

It is late September, a week before our trip, and we're prepared to go. The only thing unknown, and which we can't control, is the weather. We check all sources. The meteorological forecast looks good: a stable weather system over the Bregaglia region and sunny with a little cloud. As our departure date draws near we become more and more excited. We pack the last few things, and I manage to fit in a silk dress and shawl – just in case we finish early and go somewhere fancy for a meal.

Our flights are booked for an early Friday morning, and we're to arrive in Venice at about midday. We aim to be at the small village of Bondo to collect the permits to enter the area before the office in the village hall closes. It would also be better, for the next part of the journey, to drive up the steep mountain track in daylight. We'd then have enough light to find the path through the forests leading to the start of the six hundred metre ascent.

The Sasc Fura hut is situated high up the slope, on a prominent outcrop. The climb would normally take between two to two-and-a-half hours. Most Alpine huts are staffed by a resident guardian, either for the whole or for part of the year. Provisions are flown in by helicopter. As part of their duty, the guardians provide hot meals and act as a safety backup for climbers and walkers. They are experts on the local area and are knowledgeable about weather and snow conditions. Each hut has a visitor's book for climbers in which they write up the details of their proposed route. If a climber or walker doesn't return on time, the guardians alert rescue teams in the area.

We pack a few small luxuries to make our evening prior to the climb, and our return, more comfortable. We'll leave these in the hut.

We plan to arrive at the hut by eight or nine in the evening. It will allow enough time for us to repack our equipment into our small daypacks for the ascent the following day.

We estimate that we'll reach the top by early to mid-afternoon, enabling us enough time to make the tricky descent in daylight. Around eighty percent of climbing accidents happen on the descent, when one is tired and where one often has to rely on the safety of equipment during long and continuous abseils.

The Piz Badile is not an easy mountain to descend. Its north and east faces are sheer vertical walls of granite, almost a thousand metres' high. They are separated by a long jagged ridgeline facing north and stretch in total around a kilometre and a half, from base to summit. The descent from this side of the mountain involves multiple, technical abseils down the steep north-facing spine. For most of the descent one relies on the safety of equipment, on one's judgement, and on an ability to deal with the dangers of loose boulders, steep drops and the difficulties of regaining one's position on the ridgeline. It would definitely be advisable to embark on this descent in daylight, when we can see where we're going.

The only other descent is down the south-facing slopes. This would be a lot longer, and would require careful navigation. Descending this way would present additional logistical problems. We would need to hitch more than a hundred kilometres, skirting the southern flank of the Bregaglia range and Lake Como, then re-crossing the border into Switzerland.

The option to retrace our steps is a technically more difficult choice, but it will be quicker, logistically more simple and, consequently, safer.

Absolutely everything is ready. Now I really am excited. On Tuesday evening I stop off at the climbing wall to buy a piece of cord for my chalk bag. I meet up with a friend, an experienced climber, and tell him about our plans. Everything seems just perfect.

3   To the Alps

Remember how we came at last
To Como; shower and storm and blast
Had blown the lake beyond his limit,
And all was flooded; and how we past

....

I climb'd the roofs at break of day;
Sun-smitten Alps before me lay.
I stood among the silent statues,
And statued pinnacles, mute as they.
FROM 'THE DAISY' BY LORD ALFRED TENNYSON

The plane powers down the runway, and now I know our climbing adventure is really happening. I love adventure. I feel like the luckiest woman alive.

Everything goes according to plan. We hire a small car and travel north from Venice, reaching Lake Como in the mid afternoon. It is so beautiful. I understand why artists from the Romantic era favoured this area. Like a painting, shimmering, turquoise water reflects the snow-capped mountains; charming villages dot the lakeside. The effect of light on water is mesmerising. My mind wanders. I imagine large fish and strange creatures living in its depths.

We pass through numerous mountain tunnels. Each time we exit, Lake Como appears on our left. It begins to feel as if we aren't beside a lake at all, but beside the sea.

Architectural columns proudly introduce many of the stately facades along the lake. Sculptures adorn terraced gardens, heavy with lush vegetation. A breeze churns the blue water into checked patterns of dark and light. The pan-tiled roofs of buildings echo shapes cast by the wind on the water.

Had we more time, I would want to travel the entire one hundred and seventy kilometre circumference of the lake.

The shores of the lake are in two provinces, Como and Lecco. The lake has been a crossing point between Central Europe and the Mediterranean since Roman times, and a bridging point for communications northwards through the Alps and southwards to Rome. Here, too, the Romans built retreats and holiday villas.

At the south-western end of the lake is the city of Como, famous for its architectural and carpentry masters and its textiles. At the lake's south-eastern tip is Lecco, home of Riccardo Cassin and the Spiders of Lecco.

We continue to the very northern tip of the lake where its waters are fed by the Mera. This powerful river heads north, makes a sharp loop eastwards and at Castasegna crosses the border into Switzerland.

The road runs parallel to the river, and soon we're passing through a border post staffed by men in grey uniforms and starched fez-like caps perched precariously on their heads. We are now in Switzerland. The river cuts its way upstream through a deep-sided valley flanked by mountains – the Bregaglia Alps. Relating to their position when travelling from Italy to France via the Swiss Alps, the name derives from an ancient word meaning 'pre-Gaul'.

After about four kilometres we reach a fuel station. Beyond it a small turning to the right is marked 'Bondo'. We fill the car with fuel, and buy some snacks. There is a little coffee shop in a corner. The rich aroma of percolating coffee mingles with sweet-smelling tobacco. I place a miniature packet of salted peanuts on the counter next to some chocolate bars.

"These are not for now," I say, as Jeremy stuffs the chocolate bars into his jacket pocket. "The peanuts are for when we've done our climb."

There will only be a mouthful each, but for me there's nothing quite like filling your mouth with delicious peanuts after a tiring day in the mountains.

We climb back into our car, and take the turning to Bondo. We're nearly there.

It is late afternoon and cloudy. The combination of cloud and the high surrounding mountains make everything darker. The road becomes narrow. We follow it through tight gaps between old stone buildings. Our little car rattles over the cobbles. Finally we turn the last corner and swing into an open courtyard. An octagonal fountain decorates its centre. Before us is a church that looks as if it's a survivor from the thirteenth century. We're here to obtain a handwritten permit from an official at the local hotel before continuing our journey up the Bondasca valley.

The hotel has the most singular reception area imaginable. It looks little more than an old village hall. The building is constructed from hefty, square-cut stones, and lacks windows. We find ourselves in an ochre-coloured room with a high ceiling. It is sparsely decorated and a few glass cabinets stand uncomfortably on spindly legs along its length. They are out of place in the large room, a room that would have favoured more robust furnishings. A slight man appears from an adjoining room. I press my nose to one of the glass cabinets and study the curios. Jeremy, in a mixture of English and broken French, tries to convey to the assistant our wish to purchase permits to enter the valley beyond the village.

A couple of old postcards are propped on some faded cloth, among which is one featuring a black-and-white photograph of the Piz Badile. In the photograph the mountain is veiled in its winter cloak of snow and ice. It looks both beautiful and terrifying. It is so enormous that the crevasses in the surrounding glaciers – large enough to accommodate a mini-bus – look like hairline fractures on a china teacup. Not only is the mountain enormous, but it's dark and isolated in the picture, cut off from the alpine slopes by thick glaciers flowing like white yoghurt from the cracks where the mountain rises from the earth. The glaciers spill outwards, right to the tail of the north ridge.

"At least we won't have to worry about all that snow on the way up," I whisper to myself.

Jeremy places some Swiss francs on the table. The man behind the desk adjusts his glasses and reaches into the desk drawer. He produces a small bunch of keys. He unlocks the glass cabinet, slides a bony hand behind the glass and plucks out the postcard I've been admiring. Without expression or word he hands it to me. His fingers touch the palm of my hand. They feel like ice and, for a second, I'm not sure I want the card. I glance at Jeremy. He nods and smiles. "It would be better to get it now. The building might be locked when we return."

It's a chilly evening. Once outside, I walk briskly over the cobbled paving to the car. I look at the postcard once more, place it in the dashboard, reach across and tug at the seat belt.

"That's a really strange village. It's almost as if no one except that peculiar man lives there," I comment.

But Jeremy is focused on the road ahead and soon I, too, am absorbed in the next part of our venture. The cobbles stop abruptly and for a short stretch are replaced by potholed tar. It soon runs out. A gravel track bends sharply back on itself and leads steeply into the forest behind the village. As we ascend the track it narrows to a single lane rising steadily through the trees and looping back in many hairpin bends as we gain height. The ground to my right drops away dramatically and, as we round yet another corner, I have a clear view of the Bondasca River below. All that separates us from a great drop is ten centimetres of dubious unmade road. I edge closer to the gear stick and pray silently that we'll not skid on loose dirt. I think that if this was the kind of road Italians learn to drive on, it's no wonder they're impatient with moderate speeds on two-lane mountain passes which are tarred and have barriers.

The small car labours up the mountain track for another forty minutes before the ground levels out. Through the pines I catch a glimpse of wooden buildings. An isolated farming settlement, perhaps? A grader has cut into the earth on one side of the track, creating a dent in the road. Jeremy guides the vehicle into the hollow and turns off the engine.

It is dusk. We lift our rucksacks from the boot, pull on our head torches and make one final check before starting out.

On his recce the previous summer Jeremy had made a mental note of the starting point. "We're looking for a small pathway that leads off the track on the right, somewhere about here," he says.

A recent sprinkling of rain has dampened the knee-high undergrowth. The leaves and grass droop, covering any sign of an obvious path. We wade through thick bushes, searching for a well-used track. More than once before I have mistaken animal tracks for a man-made trail, and have ended up at the swampy bank of a river. I know that we have to get onto the main path before night falls, otherwise it will be too difficult to see anything, and we'll land up walking in circles.

Jeremy waves to indicate that he's found the way. I hurry towards him. As abruptly as the path starts, it stops. Jeremy back-tracks a few paces. Suddenly he jumps over a boulder and slides down the other side.

"Okay, this way," he says, grinning over his shoulder. His ability to find his way is uncanny.

The guidebook has suggested that from the gravel road, the journey up to the Sasc Fura hut would take a fit party around two hours. I never pay much attention to these timings. Most guidebooks are written by fit male alpinists, in the prime of their lives, who are often local guides and who know every stone. In my brain I add another hour and a half to the time, so I won't become despondent when things take longer than suggested.

Darkness falls. It's as if the mountains are asleep. Only the wind whistles through the forest, swooshing the long, pine needles, like giant brushes sweeping the slopes. I breathe in the scent of conifers and forest vegetation.

Jeremy is ahead, waiting for me in a clearing. He stands silently, a shadow in the moonlight. When I join him he points to the dark outline of the pine trees against the sky. Above the pointy tops shines the moon, partially covered by cloud and with a hazy circle of light around it. He reaches down and feels for my hand. I can't be happier or more content. I wish the moment could last forever, but at the same time eagerly anticipate the journey ahead. This is going to be the best climb of my life. I just know it.

We continue up the steep path. A yawn escapes me. I'm tired after our long journey. A large boulder looms above us. For a moment I think it might be the hut. It isn't.

"Not long now," says Jeremy, spurring me on.

I push my walking sticks deeper into the earth, lengthening my stride up the steep incline below the boulder. We're above the pine forests and without their protection the chilling air from the glaciers blows sharply over the small boulders and tufts of grass, piercing my ears and willing me forward. Wind from high mountain regions always feels like ice. It's sharp and invigorating, but not something in which to linger. The slope eases. When next I look up there is the outline of a mountain hut just a few metres ahead.

Back in London, Steve Gorton is sitting at his desk working on his latest photographic assignment. Over the past few years Steve has become a close climbing friend. He's always smiling, always keen to take up or suggest an exciting adventure to break the monotony of routine training. I constantly marvel at his youthful appearance, this despite a family with two teenage children and a hectic career. We'd met at the climbing wall a few days before Jeremy and I were to leave. I'd just bought a new lightweight waterproof, and he'd been commenting on my purchase.

STEVE

It was Friday and I'd just finished going through my list of photographic assignments for the following week. The kids were watching TV and Julie, my wife, was reading. I was browsing the web. Out of curiosity I flicked to the European forecast for the Bregaglia region where Rachel and Jeremy were headed. I don't know why, but I just had an uneasy feeling.

Rachel had said the weather looked good, but things can change quite quickly. I felt a shudder down my spine when I read, "Intense storm activity imminent, electric storms and gale-force cyclonic low to move in Saturday p.m. Outlook beyond Monday uncertain."

The forecast must have changed since I'd spoken to Rachel. This was predicting two or three days of extreme storm activity. I was concerned. I had never seen a forecast like this for this region. What if they hadn't received the update?

I joined the kids watching a sitcom, but all the time I had a nagging feeling at the back of my mind. What if they had left before the weather report was updated? Perhaps I was the only one who knew what they were heading into. But then, I thought, they would get an update from the guardian at the mountain hut, so I was probably just being over-anxious.

Later that evening I sent a phone message. I didn't want to alarm them. It's just that when you've lost friends in the mountains you become a bit more edgy about these things. "Hi Rachel, Jeremy. There's an unexpected change in the weather. It's not looking good. Just think you should know." There was no reply, but then at 10 p.m., with a big climb ahead, they would probably be snoring their heads off by now.

4   Our own chalet

As in any alpine region, the weather is changeable, protection questionable, route-finding bewildering, rockfall frequent and descents tedious. In short, it's everything you could ever ask for.
THE CANADIAN ALPINE JOURNAL, 1993

There is no light inside the mountain hut. As we approach everything is still. My poles clatter as I move up the steps to the entrance. The entrance porch is made from Alpine pine. A barometer hangs from a large beam. It reads over a thousand millibars, suggesting favourable conditions – good for the climb tomorrow. The weather forecast has been accurate. So far everything is in place. And we had almost made the 'guidebook time' of two hours to the hut. It's strange, though, that everything is so dark. Even though it's a quieter time of the year, the guardian normally leaves a light on as a beacon. It's around 10 p.m. Where is everyone? They should be clearing up. Perhaps they've all gone to bed early, in readiness for the day ahead?

Jeremy pulls the door handle. It doesn't move. He tries opening the door by pushing his shoulder against it in case it's merely stiff. It remains firmly locked.

I put my face to the window, try to peer through cracks, but can't see anything. We bang on the door in case the guardian is there by himself, but the banging echoes back. No one ... The only thing that moves is the water trickling into a trough outside. Some of the huts close early in the season. I guess it's just our luck to have reached one of those. Funny, though. There wasn't mention of this in the guidebook, but then things change over time, and sometimes written information is inaccurate.

Jeremy tries the handle again. I go off in search of another entrance. The cold stone stairs seem our best bivi option but, as a last resort, I push my fingers behind one of the window frames. Perhaps one of these hasn't been closed properly and we might be able to open it. Nothing budges. Well, it wouldn't be the first time I've slept outside an alpine hut.

It is going to be a chilly night, but I don't mind. We'll curl up together in the doorway. It won't be the most comfortable night, but certainly more so than many nights that I've spent alone in snowy mountains. I've always liked being on my own in wilderness and mountain areas, but having someone to share it with is so much more fun ... especially someone I fancy.

Jeremy leaves me for a few minutes. I walk to one of the drinking troughs. A little fountain trickles in fresh water from the mountain stream. At the other end a small pipe trails the overflow out onto the stones. I splash my face, and dig into my rucksack for a cloth. After a reasonable dousing in the most essential places, it's time for a small reward for completing the walk to the hut, and for braving the cold water and night air in the name of cleanliness. I sit in the entrance area and open the top pocket of my rucksack. I've only half-finished munching on the chocolate bar when Jeremy re-appears. He reaches for my hand and asks me to follow. Fifty metres away from the main refuge stands another, smaller, wooden building that appears to be an outhouse. I'm slightly surprised when Jeremy pushes the door open and waves me inside. I stuff the last handful of chocolate into my mouth.

The floorboards creak as we enter. Ahead is a small window, presumably with a view of the Piz Cengalo and Piz Badile. To our right is a small bunk-bed, the top bunk so high that you'd be unable to sit up straight in bed without banging your head on the wooden ceiling. A table occupies one corner. In another is a wood-burning stove. Magic! Our own little chalet, high in the Swiss Alps.

I suggest we sleep on the top bunk. It's always more fun high off the ground. There's no time to waste. Both of us are tired from the long journey. Tomorrow we'll have to move before the sun pokes its nose over the mountains. We roll out our sleeping bags. I drift to sleep with the sound of the wind and the warmth of Jeremy's body in the sleeping bag beside me.

The alarm clock sounds out in the dark, heralding the start of the next phase of our adventure. In the moonlight are the shapes of our rucksacks and equipment, laid ready. It's cold. I'm slightly nauseous. Perhaps it's in nervous anticipation of our climb, or perhaps it's because we've climbed nearly two thousand metres in altitude since leaving London the day before. I lie still for a moment. The feeling of nausea is not unfamiliar; it's something I've experienced many times before doing a big climb: that feeling of fear that accompanies the excitement of a journey into the unknown. There's always an element of uncertainty in technical climbing, no matter how well prepared you might be. In my mind I go through our preparation and planning. I try to create a mental picture of the mountain close up to give me the confidence of putting fifteen years' experience into practice.

The postcard on the dashboard, and that strange man who'd handed it to me, keep popping into my thoughts. I have an uneasy feeling. A premonition? But, sometimes thinking too much doesn't help. One just has to get on with it.

We're soon up and readying ourselves, measuring liquid carbohydrate drinks into containers and discussing what last few items we might need. Jeremy uses the blade from his helmet to remove some pages which we'll need for the climb from the guidebook.

There are a few things that don't fit into the daypacks and we'll have to leave them behind. These are spread out on the lower bunk in the hope there might be space for one or two more pieces once everything else is packed. Among them is my mobile phone. I'd charged it in the car en route and had added extra call time credit, just in case of an emergency. However, in the mountains I've been unable to get reception and it seems extremely improbable we'll find a signal high on the north face of such a large mountain. I flip the phone up and down in my hand a couple of times, assessing whether, if I find a space, the additional weight will be worth the effort. Eventually I find a small gap alongside my gloves and stuff it inside. It's time to go. I push the remaining items into the top of the larger rucksack, which is staying behind. The last task is to fasten our harnesses and attach the metal bits of climbing paraphernalia to them. The equipment jangles like a suit of armour as we move. We're like two warriors prepared for battle. Now I feel ready.

We leave the cabin, our head torches lighting the way. Jeremy jangles ahead. I push hard to keep up. This is no time to be feeble and let the side down, and anyway I don't fancy losing my way in the dark.

At first the path leads through a few alpine conifers behind the main hut. Then it bounces back and forth over a small stream. It's a steady uphill climb and after a while the landscape changes to stony rubble interspersed with large smooth boulders marked by glacial scarring. It isn't long before dawn breaks, exposing the gigantic north-east face ahead of us, a sheer wall of granite that would intimidate any climber. In geology this zone marks the northern and western boundary of the southern Alps. It's a natural fault line along which different rock types were pushed together.

The mountain is flanked on the left by a couloir separating it from the Cengalo peak. To the right the cliff extends to meet the great north ridge, creating a sharp crest that stands like a cardboard cut-out against the early morning sky. It drops away sharply on both sides. A huge area of spires, edges and folds extends from the summit of the Badile to where it merges into the plains below.

This is what we'll be climbing today. We'll need to move quickly to cover all the ground in just one day. It's over a thousand metres of ascent, separated into technical climbing pitches of around fifty metres. The guidebook suggests that a swiftly-moving party may be able to climb this in a single, long day. This would mean not making any mistakes, or resting along the way.

Long alpine routes require enduring focus and will. There is probably nothing more daunting than being confronted with a lifetime's worth of grey granite, and realising that even though you cannot see the end of it, you're going to have to push, pull and haul your way to the top. The process is exhausting and seemingly endless. The further you move from the comforts of the valley below and into the unknown above, the less option there is to turn back. Each metre upwards means another level of commitment, thrusting you further into the challenge. There's no room for wavering. Lack of concentration and focus has cost many people their lives.

The sun pokes over the tips of the mountains to the east. The peak ahead looks like a massive sleeping dragon, its tail curving down towards us, the sharp points of the crest igniting like flames, one after the other.

The Piz Badile's northern side is separated from the approaching slopes by a permanent glacier. This adds difficulty to its accessibility. To the east lies the Trubinasca Glacier and to the west the Cengalo Glacier. We scramble up alongside the snout of the Trubinasca Glacier.

The natural sounds of the higher regions of the European Alps are so different from those of the savannah plains and deep kloofs of the highveld in South Africa. Long before the highveld dawn breaks, the new day is signalled by a bird chorus, and even late into the night one hears the sounds of animals out on the prowl. Here, amongst the glaciers and moraine slopes, things are still, the silence pierced only by the frightening sound of avalanches – tons of snow and boulders cascading down the huge slopes.

The terrain is inhospitable to most animals, and is inhabited only by hardy creatures able to survive prolonged periods of freezing weather and feeding on scant vegetation. Perhaps, if we're lucky, we'll see one of the mountain marmots, similar to the rock dassies found on Table Mountain in Cape Town – though marmots are a lot larger and fatter than dassies. Once I came across a herd of chamois in the forested lower slopes of Mont Blanc. I'd followed their tracks in the snow for an hour or two and then saw them grazing in a hollow between two ravines. I know it was a lucky sighting. Most visitors to the Alps never glimpse these beautiful creatures.

We scramble up the easy-angled slabs west of the true ridge, to get to where it joins the north spine slightly higher up. I look down and see the very tip of the glacier. A trickle of water exits it, joining with other trickles to form a small stream. It is in itself is a deeply satisfying experience to have traced the origins of Lake Como right back along the Mera and Bondasca rivers to its source.

The scrambling becomes more vertical. Eventually the walking poles become a hindrance. We pull through a chimney onto the crest of the ridge. We prop the poles upright in a prominent place near the exit of the crest – if our climb takes longer than anticipated, we can shine torches down the ridge as we abseil off it, the reflection from the poles showing us where to go.

I shiver, for a moment contemplating what would happen if we abseiled down one of the subsidiary ridgelines, mistaking it for the correct route back. Here large crevasses open like traps. Many climbers have slipped and lost their lives in that world below the satin covering of snow. Preserved and frozen, their bodies push slowly down, exiting the snout years later, fully clothed, roped and with equipment still hanging about them.

I reflect on what it is that drives me on. One thing I try to do is focus on having a positive attitude, and not on failure. For instance, if you're climbing a sheer cliff, your body will literally freeze if you think about losing your footing and dragging your partner down with you. The power of the imagination to exert a chemical and physical change over the body is remarkable. Experience teaches you to read these physical changes, and to work out what thoughts might have woken them. In so doing you're able to retrace your steps and reorganise your thoughts.

Often the mind is so powerful that you're able to convince yourself to follow an illogical course of action, even when the pitfalls are obvious. Sometimes it takes a great deal of self-discipline and commitment to go against a solution which appears to provide short-term relief, in favour of the long-term goal, or of safety. From experience I know our ascent is simply a methodical process of inching our way, little by little, until we've achieved our objective safely.

We scramble further up the lower sections. Finally, the mountain directs us to its first test.

5 The climb

There is a region of heart's desire
Free for the hand that wills;
land of the shadow and haunting spire,
land of the silvery glacier fire,
land of the cloud and the starry choir,
magical land of hills;
loud with the crying of winds and streams,
thronged with the fancies and fears of dreams.
GEOFFREY WINTHROP YOUNG

We pick our way up the easier sections for about forty-five minutes. The ascent has been well within our capabilities. Some people rope up for such a section, and then separate the climb into pitches. This would mean that they'd be travelling more slowly which, in the long run, might not be as safe. The longer you remain on the route, the greater the chance of being caught in bad weather, or of falling prey to stone fall, or to accidents caused by fatigue. For us, this section is quicker unroped, there being no hindrance of a rope dragging over the spikes and edges between us.

From my exposed position, I take a moment to look down and, in doing so, experience that familiar sensation of vertigo. It makes me grip a little tighter. I try not to look at where I might land if I make a mistake. The outcrop steepens. Jeremy pauses. Now seems a good time to loosen the coils tied to our backs and to fasten a shortened length between us.

"Happy to uncoil the ropes here?" Jeremy asks.

Carefully I wedge a metal chock into a fissure in the granite and fasten myself to it. I lean back slowly, lifting the rope off my back and tying one end to my harness. It smells new, more reassuring than the old, furry ropes I used as a beginner climber at university. With a short line between us, we'll be able to cover ground quickly. Maybe even be on top by early afternoon. This would be ideal. We'll be able to make the initial tricky descent in daylight.

We wrap the spare coils over our shoulders and tie them off. To give us extra security we allow twelve metres to loop over spikes and cracks as we climb.

The sun is well up. I lead towards the lighter arête above. For a few hours we move in tandem, weaving between boulders, over bulges, spires and tricky blank faces. The only sounds are the clink of our metal equipment and the breeze through the mountains. As the technical difficulty increases, we unravel spare coils, allowing one of us to move ahead to negotiate tricky sections.

It is sunny and crisp. A light breeze grows as we climb. Fresh mountain air tingles in my nose. The excitement of nearly reaching the summit makes me smile. Jeremy's eyes sparkle deep blue. He, too, looks energised by our accomplishments. I reach forward and smear up the next smooth section of rock. Near the top the mountain gives way to large boulders, some pushed neatly together, others seeming only a touch away from cascading down its face. Heaving over an awkward bulge, I push down hard to stand up on a large, cupboard-size block. The entire block groans and shifts. It would take only a fraction of it to squash me. Quickly I flick the ropes to one side and tiptoe passed. Slightly rattled, I point at the oblong chunk,

"If we come back this way we need to watch that."

I think Jeremy senses my fear. His reply is a reassuring nod and a broad grin.

I'm hoping now we might descend the less vertical terrain on the other side of the mountain. It will involve some precise navigation, but there'll be fewer abseils and less chance of a problem.

Many people hire alpine guides to lead them safely to places they would otherwise find inaccessible. For a fee, guides provide planning, logistics, route-finding and leadership. My work involves training individuals and groups in climbing, sometimes organising guides or leading parties myself on tailor-made climbing expeditions. It's fun to be back in the mountains again, making decisions, discussing the route finding and analysing the safety and logistics for our own climb.

The valley is a distant speck below. We're able to see the last few obstacles before the summit crest. We're working perfectly as a team. Soon I'll be gazing south to the plains of northern Italy, to the land connecting it to the jagged spires of the Swiss Alps. I laugh out aloud. It's great this sense of being free.

I sprint up the next section. The gain of nearly another thousand metres in altitude makes me wheeze. I reach Jeremy breathless, but ready for the next part of the ascent. He's belayed on top of a pointy outcrop. Ahead is a ramp of near vertical snow extending upward for around fifteen metres. It's my turn to lead off. Suddenly it doesn't seem so appealing.

It would waste time kitting up in gloves and overtrousers just for a small section covered in snow. Beyond, the route becomes rocky again, and I would then have take off the thick gloves and change back into my rock-climbing shoes for the small granite features ahead.

At any rate it would be prudent to keep my approach shoes dry for the descent, which will be partly at night when the temperature might drop well below freezing.

There's no easy way to wriggle out of what is my lead. I guess it could be an opportunity to impress. After all, we're on a date, and I feel duty bound to do my best.

Quickly I march through the snow, trying not to appear unwilling. The temperature has cooled with the ascent and, for the snow to have remained in the slight depression, it must be just above zero

The start is relatively easy; the snow is just calf deep. As the angle increases, I find myself wading, finally floundering. I try to swim across the banked-up section, eventually shoving my arms deep into the thick, white barricade to try to gain some purchase. The trailing ropes drag me down as I push upwards. It becomes an ungainly, gasping struggle. A rather bemused Jeremy looks on patiently from his perch. We hadn't been expecting this much snow on something that is usually a rock climb.

At last I reach a protruding granite pinnacle. Flushed and humbled by my clumsy efforts, I tug at the boulder to make sure it's still firmly attached to the mountain, and then lasso it. Taking the slack rope in around the rock, I bring Jeremy across. He makes it all look quite easy, and climbs onwards, tentatively working his way up the icy section above.

"Good lead!" he says, encouragingly.

I can't help but think my inelegant efforts are being somewhat surpassed. I'm beginning to feel I've had enough. Knee-deep in ice particles, with a biting wind and numb feet, the whole thing is less than pleasant. But it won't be long before it's over. It's now become a case of shutting up and getting on with it. Not every moment of a climb can be fun or heroic.

From that point on everything is coated in verglas ice, linked by patches of snow. In our climbing shoes, usually the appropriate footwear for a rock climb, it's becoming a near impossible task. Our progress is slowing considerably. Instead of taking fifteen minutes to climb a section, we're now taking around forty minutes. The temperature is a couple of degrees cooler than we'd hoped but, even if we had lugged up heavy mountaineering boots, axes and crampons, they would have been pretty useless on the thin smattering of slippery ice that coats the rocks.

I catch up with Jeremy on the next section. He's stopped short of an upright wall, about twenty metres high. Cloaked in a layer of glossy ice, it towers above us like a perpendicular skating rink. It is impossible to ascend. Beyond, I see the boulders curving round the summit ridge. They're just out of reach. We're so close – thirty vertical metres from placing our hands on the summit cairn.

Had the conditions been just a couple of degrees warmer, the ice on the rock wall ahead of us would have melted. Although it might have been damp, with our rock shoes we'd have been able to inch our way up this last slab, by smearing on the wall. Now our path onward is blocked. Not only can we not see the summit, there is no longer the option of taking the gentler route down the other side of the mountain.

This last pitch was mentioned briefly in the guide. It was described simply as the last technical section before the summit scramble. There was no mention of the possibility of verglas. Now we'll have to return down the north ridge.

We prepare our equipment for the return journey abseiling down the ridge. The descent will take hours. There'll be tricky abseils all the way.

If we'd been able to reach the top we'd have been able to see across the Italian plains. We'd also have seen the build-up of thick cumulus clouds heading in our direction, forming the greatest storm experienced in the Bregaglia region in recent times.

6 No margin for error

And up on the mountain we began our ant-like labours. What is a man on an ice-world up in the sky ...

GASTON RÉBUFFAT

On the South African highveld around Johannesburg, there's always a warning before a thunderstorm. A breeze catches at the dry grass. It builds quickly, providing relief from the oppressive heat. Birds dart between trees chirping, not gently as in the early mornings, but in distressed, sharp tones. The last few minutes before the storm are silent. The wind dies. Everything is quiet. Large clouds hang, waiting until the first clap of thunder heralds the downpour – a symphony of rain, thunder and lightning. The storm lasts an hour, maybe two, before sweeping away. Everything emerges newly washed, glistening, and the 'rainbird', Burchell's Coucal, gurgles like the sound of a waterfall.

Rock climbing in the Magaliesberg mountains to the north of Johannesburg taught me to recognise these signs and take cover, usually below a rock overhang, until the downpour had finished.

I was soon to learn that alpine storms are very different. They sneak in behind the high mountains and descend without warning. Gale-force winds, terrifying lightning strikes and torrential downpours of rain, hail and snow may last days, sometimes weeks. Once trapped you are isolated. It becomes a battle for life. Few live to tell the tale.

The wind suddenly picks up. Within minutes the temperature plummets. From hovering just around freezing, it's now a good few degrees below that. Thick cloud swirls around us, cutting off our view of the valley. It's as if the cloud has come from nowhere, just appearing around the edges of the mountain. This weather wasn't forecast. I'm frightened by the sudden change. At around 4 p.m. we're at the centre of a violent electric storm.

"We need to get off here now!" For the first time Jeremy is anxious.

There's a resounding crack of thunder, like the blow of an axe. A talon of pink lightning arcs across the sky. I know it's too late.

"This isn't good. It isn't good," Jeremy mutters

I look about me. We're on the crest of a long ridge, covered in metal climbing equipment and tied to a metal fixing in the mountain. We're like two pylons inviting the lightning to strike. Thunder booms. Neon light zigzags around us. Our entire descent will be following the exposed crest. There'll be no shelter, no safe place to hide.

Hanging from our harnesses, we dive into rucksacks for waterproof jackets, overtrousers, gloves and hats. We fasten torches to our heads. It's going to be a long night, and this will probably be the last opportunity to stop. From now on our hands will be on the ropes, either pulling them through the abseil device, flicking the ends out of cracks, or flaking coils for the next abseil.

Large flakes of snow quickly cover exposed features on the rocky surface. The wind is so strong it's difficult for us to hear each other. With a deafening crack a huge jagged bolt of lightning strikes beside me. I shake with fear and adrenaline. The next one will be sure to hit.

At least I'm not alone. It would be so easy to panic, and lose control.

To make sure everything is fastened correctly and we're pulling the right line at the end, we yell out our checklist for the abseil. We need to drive fear from our minds, to keep our wits about us if we're going to get out of here alive.

The vast majority of mountaineering fatalities happen on the descent, most often in abseil. Jeremy and I have both lost a best friend in abseiling accidents, one in Patagonia, the other in Canada. We know of others, too – of how easily experienced mountaineers have perished in this way. We will need to rely on each other and on every detail being correct. One mistake will be one mistake too many.

Jeremy moves down steadily, watching each step. I hang off the mountain. The lightning sizzles nearby releasing pungent ozone into the air. I'm reminded that we also lost a climbing associate to lightning on an expedition to Elbrus in the Caucasus in Russia. My brother, Julian, had a close shave when the electric current from a bolt that struck his shelter, radiated down the sides and caught the edge of his exposed right foot. He'd returned home with a large white streak across it.

I want to untie from the ring, to race down the lines, but I have to wait my turn. My heart is pounding.

Jeremy reaches the next stance. The lines slacken. I can't hear the cry of "Ropes free" – which would mean he's completed his abseil and I can now fasten myself to the lines, but I'm waiting no longer.

I attach my belay device to my harness and lower myself. Gale-force winds tear over the ridge. I have difficulty from being swept off my feet. My shoes slide on the verglassed rocks and mounds of fresh snow, and my feet are numb. Wind whips round my face. Snow and hail sting my nose and cheeks. Strands of loose hair catch passing snowflakes that stick and form matted globules. I know I have to ignore the discomfort and get on with the descent.

I push the ropes carefully through the abseil device and move down a little further. Each movement is slow and deliberate. Every couple of metres I look up to make sure the ropes are correctly lined up and are not going to pull any loose rocks on top of me. It's a slow process, and I'm relieved when I see Jeremy's red jacket, his familiar features. Everything seems to be taking so much longer to organise in the gale. Daylight is quickly fading. I switch on my head torch.

He's now just a few metres below, hanging in his harness, waiting patiently for me to finish the slow descent. I reach down and clip myself to the anchor. The metal of the carabiner is stuck to my gloves. Jeremy unties the knotted ends of rope.

"We're pulling on pink, aren't we?" he yells over the wind.

"Pulling on pink," I shout back.

He tugs at the pink rope. It slithers down the snowy face. The yellow end snakes upward. Automatically we flatten against the cliff face, tuck our arms in, and squash our necks and helmets into our shoulders. The knot in the rope often pulls down debris as it plummets towards you.

This time we're showered only with loose snow. Jeremy picks through the frozen tangle. I pull the pink end through the next ring.

Together we chant a rhyme: "Pull on yellow, fellow, pull on yellow." It reminds us which end to tug the next time round. Pulling on the wrong rope can cause the knot to jam as it squeezes through the metal ring. In snowy conditions it will freeze tight. One person would then have to climb all the way back up to the free end of the rope. We can't afford such a mishap.

Before tossing the ends over the edge, we tie a large knot in the last part of the rope, to prevent us abseiling off the end. Jeremy then rappels down the lines. I'm left on the stance. My feet are now hard, white and dead. I reach down to rub them, to regain the circulation. My overtrousers keep slipping down under the harness. My jacket hitches up each time I bend. The wind whistles up my spine. I shiver.

A high-pitched hum reverberates through the air. At first I dismiss it as being nerves getting the better of me. The humming intensifies. It sounds like bees making a hive in my helmet. It reaches deafening proportions, drowning out the gale. My head feels as if it's about to explode. Lightning has turned everything an eerie, shadowless pink. The flashes are followed by violent crashes of thunder. Then all goes dark. My head torch is off. I think it must have got wet and reach up to switch it back on. It lights up immediately. There seems to be nothing wrong with it. I abseil to the next stance. As I approach Jeremy, the noise in my head starts again.

"Can you hear that?" I yell.

By the time I'm next to him the sound is intense. I strain to hear his answer.

"I thought it was you." He looks worried.

I feel as if something terrible is about to happen. My helmet vibrates again. The sky explodes in light and sound. This time both our head torches die. We begin to realise they're being charged by the electricity in the atmosphere. At any moment we could become human lightning conductors as it earths itself through our bodies.

Jeremy is trying to find the ends of the two ropes.

"I'll flake this one," he yells over the storm, reaching for the yellow cord.

We can't just give up, so we work together, our hoods touching as we check the knots and prepare our exit. Jeremy moves off. His nylon overtrousers are alive with static sparks. If the situation weren't so serious, it would have been an impressive, impromptu fireworks display. Now it's become part of a developing personal horror story.

I start to think about whether or not we'll die. I estimate we probably have less than a thirty per cent chance of getting out alive, but if we're struck it'll be a quick death. All sorts of horrific thoughts tumble through my mind: if one of us were struck by lightning, would the electricity transmit down the wet rope and kill the other? What will happen if one of us survives and is left up here alone?

I can't let my mind wander like this. My hands tremble. I feel nauseous and weak. I swallow hard and bite my lower lip as the atmosphere displays its amazing lightshow. I look down and see Jeremy's figure far below as he struggles on a razor-sharp ridge, the red of his waterproofs dulled by the light. He's slipping, regaining his footing, then slipping again as the ropes stretch down to him in a long diagonal line. If he loses control, his ropes will drag him over the sheer sides. He'll be battered, hanging almost twenty metres out of reach. My mind wills him to stay focused, calm, not to fall.

Each time the lightning strikes I'm thankful we've been spared. After a few hours, reaching up to switch our head torches back on just becomes part of the procedure. We work as quickly as we can setting up the next rappel, then the next one. Methodically, at each belay station every fifty metres or so, Jeremy pulls out the small, crumpled piece of guidebook from his pocket, and we try to work out where we are.

"I think we're here now," he says.

"Hang on, Jeremy ... I remember a piece of red climbing tape hanging from an old piton near the belay station. Are you sure we've reached that point?"

"Look around you, Rachel, the snow has covered everything. The red tape is probably lying under a mound of snow."

As our ropes start to freeze, the task of threading becomes harder each time. Our hands work clumsily through the thick gloves.

"Check my knot," Jeremy yells above the wind.

It's a simple overhand with two long tails. We can only hope that each time we tighten it enough, and that we leave a long enough tail of ropes so it doesn't slide undone as we lower ourselves down its length.

I can see the flicker of his head torch, a halo in the hood of his jacket, reflecting on his helmet. Below is a drop where the sharp ridge leads down about six metres to a vertical drop, a few metres over some boulders. Below this there appears to be a small bank of snow before the next rocky drop. With caution Jeremy shuffles along the ridge towards the boulders. The wind is buffeting from both sides and he has to take care not to lose his footing. He looks above to check the line of his abseil, to ensure it's running smoothly and not cutting through any deep or sharp crevices.

I'm now beyond frightened. The beam of my head torch catches the flurry of snow mixed with hail, as it falls, swirls and splatters against the cliff face above me. The ropes shift and jerk as Jeremy works his way down the lines. Looking down I think I recognise one of boulders below. I can't be sure. They're covered in snow. Jeremy crouches, lowers his body over the edge. I try hard to remember why I recognise this boulder. Suddenly it dawns on me. I shout as hard as I can.

"Watch your ropes on the rock."

The wind is too strong. Another crack of thunder rolls overhead. I yell more loudly as I watch Jeremy slide his ropes across the loose cupboard-sized boulder. He's been moving quite quickly, but for a moment he stands still and looks up, studying the line of his ropes. His head torch glistens on the snow and ice above.

"Leave your ropes! Don't flick your ropes!"

I've filled my lungs and yelled. It's hopeless. I'm tied to the stance and am watching horror playing itself out without being able to do anything about it. We're only metres apart, but there's quite literally nothing I can do. He looks. For a moment I'm relieved. He shouts something, but I can't hear. I point to the teetering block. In a last effort I fill my lungs.

It's too late. He's pushed away with both feet, and his body begins to swing back. The ropes flick. In slow motion they curl round the edge, creating a lever. It doesn't take much. The boulder tumbles towards him. I close my eyes. There's an almighty crash, and then multiple crashes as it bounces down the mountain, breaking into smaller pieces as it goes. A tingling sensation warms my fingertips. I feel sick. I wish it were all a dream. The wind wails. The snow stings my face. I'm too scared to open my eyes. I know I can't stand here all night. I take a deep breath, expecting the worst.

JEREMY

I had sparks coming from my trousers and so was abseiling fairly speedily. We were in a very exposed place and I thought the lower we got the less risk there would be of being struck by lightning. The lightning would be striking the summit pinnacles so there would be more activity close to the top. We needed to move quickly.

I remembered climbing past a loose block somewhere on this pitch, and that we had discussed this on the way up. I moved over a vertical drop to the left of a few large blocks. I had a sense the boulders above were loose and that the ropes might dislodge one of them. It reminded me of a job I'd had when I was eighteen, some fifteen years back. I'd worked in a quarry where we'd had to dislodge large boulders with crowbars, whilst on abseil. One of the workers was crushed by a boulder and the quarry was subsequently closed.

Carefully I moved back right to stay on the ridgeline. It all happened very quickly. I saw what looked like a plasma screen television hurtling towards me. My natural reactions took over. I kicked out my legs and swung my hips to push myself out to one side. The boulder whizzed passed my left shoulder and smashed a metre below me, with pieces bouncing off down the mountain. I could smell the acrid scent produced when rock shatters, and thought I needed to be more careful. I was thankful I had taken the time to put my prussic on the ropes because, had I been hit, I would have lost control of the ropes.

Jeremy looks shocked, then makes a gesture with his hands and continues down the ropes. My turn. I take extra care lining my ropes up. Dislodging one big block can mean more loose debris raining down on our heads.

It's dark. Between the electric flashes everything is black. My head torch only lights up the area directly in front of me. Anything beyond is a flurry of snow particles. As I move down the ropes, I talk to myself:

"Okay, large flat block, I remember that, it was difficult to lead." Then round the corner and down a few steps. "That's it, Rachel, come on girl."

I try to remember as much as I can of our climb down so I can keep track of where we are. It's a technique I learned from my climbing days in South Africa, when it wasn't uncommon to be benighted in steep-sided gorges, or kloofs. We would have to find our way out in the dark, sometimes sharing a head torch. Reminding myself of where I am gives me a bit of control in an otherwise chaotic situation.

We meet at the next abseil, and then the next one. By now I can't remember how many we've done, or how far we've gone. We try keeping count, but it's so difficult when you feel every minute your life is literally hanging on the edge. We pause a moment. Our minds are thinking more or less the same thing. Have we passed the two diamond-shaped boulders or not? Where were the Red Arrow Rocks? How far have we actually come?

It's important to stay on the main ridgeline, as there are heavily crevassed glaciers on both sides of an impenetrable bergschrund. It would be easy to start abseiling off a subsidiary ridge and then land up hanging in space with no way out and no way up. With ice axes, crampons and ice screws, a climber might stand a chance, but in ultra-light rock-climbing kit it will be impossible. The exposure will kill us if we stop.

Our head torches point upwards almost simultaneously. The two beams scour the surrounding rock faces, seeking a clue by which we might be guided. We study cracks stuffed full with fresh snow and ice. We stare at the shape of rocks on the night skyline, trying to recall features among the hundreds we'd memorised on the journey up. Was there an old piton somewhere? Had we missed a faded nylon sling draped round a boulder? The rock is a web of shimmering patterns and hoarfrost from snow that's landed and frozen almost instantly. It would be so easy to fool our minds into making features around us fit our memories and the rough sketch in hand.

We still haven't moved. I've lost all sensation in my feet. I'm afraid I might no longer be able to take a step, that I'll fall over. I don't mention this to Jeremy. I imagine his experience is similar. We still can't see which way to go. Finally, reluctantly, we knot the free ends of the ropes together and cast them out into the darkness.

Every minute spent searching or fumbling with equipment, is another minute wasted – and minutes can become hours. Fatigue, hunger and frustration slow one down even further. Even with experience it's sometimes difficult to assess the balance between necessary speed and dangerous haste.

I see the slow rhythmic jerk on the ropes as Jeremy moves down. Each time he moves his prussic further down the frozen lines, feeding his rope through the belay device, two grooves cut deeper into the snow near my foot. I stare in a kind of trance as the zigzag patterns of the ropes move back and forth. The wind is biting round my ankles and I shove my feet deeper into the snow where the wind can't get at them. The sky becomes illuminated with lightning and I look around quickly to take in the surrounding features. The ropes bounce back, slacken. Jeremy is off the lines. I bang the purple prussic against my sleeve to clear it of ice, and prepare to go.

The ropes are frozen and a bit thin for the abseil device, which would have suited a wider diameter. There is less friction against the metal surface than there should be, making it difficult to control the rate at which I lower myself down the lines. My hands ache from trying to grip the ropes and the prussic. I try to move smoothly, but every now and again the ropes slip and I feel myself hurtling downwards. I stop and slowly try to move down, but then it happens all over again. I bang my foot against something and, for a moment, forget to brake the rope back. My body picks up speed. "God, don't let me go."

7 The black abyss

Fear doesn't exist anywhere except in the mind.
DALE CARNEGIE

It seems ages before I reach the end of the ropes. At first it's down into darkness, then finally I'm following the beacon of light cast from Jeremy's head torch. At times my face is close to large prongs of frozen rock, the icy air burns my lungs. The winds whip snow particles into a swirling, stinging mass. Thunder continues to shake the mountain. Despite the layers of long johns, thermal trousers and breathable waterproof overtrousers, the arctic temperatures numb my legs.

Nothing is working fluidly. I'm frustrated and overwhelmed.

I lower myself down to a vertical sheet of ice. Some metres below, the face scoops away to form a large overhang. Jeremy dangles a short distance above the lip.

Neither of us wish to linger in such an inhospitable place, and we quickly reorganise the ropes so we can exit swiftly.

I feel we've reached the point of 'when' – no longer 'if' – a disaster happens. Serious accidents in the mountains are seldom the consequence of a single event. They are normally a series of smaller occurrences that build along the way. It might be because of a technical problem with ropes, because of deteriorating weather, because of nightfall limiting vision, or from getting lost, or from fatigue causing impaired judgement. A fatal incident is merely the last in a long series of events.

After eighteen hours on the go, and with freezing temperatures and a blizzard, we're physically and mentally drained. Even with the time added for delays, we should have been back in the hut, or just about reaching it. As the weather conditions continue to deteriorate, safety is increasingly slipping from our grasp.

We had started on a climb well within our competencies, and for which we'd prepared meticulously. Despite this, our preparations are being tested beyond the limit.

I slump back in my harness, tiredness washes over me. I have to stop my mind wandering. To keep alert I roll my eyes around and take deep breaths. Everything is a struggle. I'm hungry, thirsty, tired. I try sucking some carbohydrate liquid from my drinking tube. Despite the container being insulated inside my rucksack, it's become frozen. Hunger is cast to the back of my mind.

Jeremy reaches into his jacket for the page giving us basic information on the route. We try to match the information with where we are on the mountain. Nothing corresponds. We aim our head torches out into the night. Only the flurry of fast-falling snow shines back. We're confused and afraid. Intricate vertical navigation with compasses is not much use either. There don't appear to be too many options, so I recommend the most obvious one – straight down.

There is no telling what lies beyond the cliff scooped away beneath us. One thing is certain, though – we can't hang here all night. We'll die from exposure. We drop our ropes and hope for the best.

As Jeremy lowers himself, he looks up at me. I can see right into his eyes. They are dark and worried. It makes my stomach churn.

"Good luck." I put on my bravest smile and hope he can't see how uneasy I am.

He slides steadily to the lip, leans out, and swings silently over it. The last to disappear is the red hood of his jacket.

I rub my hands together and try to keep my mind occupied. The wind buffets me. I pull my hood tighter to keep my ears from aching. In the torchlight I watch my breath rise and quickly disperse into the wind. I look at the slings securing me to the face, dig my hands deeper into my jacket pockets, searching for a bit more warmth. It's very lonely and I need all the comfort I can find. Twenty minutes pass. The ropes are still taut. What is keeping him?

I think of my parents in their home in Cape Town. What will they be doing now? They'd probably spent the evening on the porch looking out at the Milky Way. Hopefully they're tucked up in bed sound asleep.

I think of my brother Julian. Is he looking down at me from above? As small children we had been best friends, and throughout our years of growing up had remained very close. Then, when he was twenty-two, he died in a car accident, and I felt like my world had shattered, that there was a huge void that could never be filled. Now, isolated from all other contact, I feel the void more intensely. Thinking he may be here in spirit comforts me. I wonder what he might say to me if we could talk to each other.

My mind returns to our situation. I hope that in a little while we'll find a sheltered place, and that the storm will pass. I imagine us warming our limbs. We'd have food to eat, and a hot cup of tea. I feel my hands wrapped around the heated plastic of the cup, the steam soothing the ravished skin on my nose and cheeks. We'd recall the adventures of tonight, reliving our moments of fear and deliberation, analysing our equipment – where it worked well, where to make improvements in the future. We'd go home thankful for the everyday things we normally take for granted.

But thirty minutes later, a thick layer of snow has coated my body as if I were part of the mountain. I don't know where Jeremy is, or if he's okay. It's difficult not to break down, because in my heart I know my family and friends are oblivious to our situation. We won't have a warm place to shelter. There'll be no food, no warm drink. If we're lucky there may be an icy perch we can curl up on. Even that is a hopeful wish. At the moment we aren't even sure we're going in the right direction. Again and again I remind myself how far we've come, how everything has worked out well despite what's happened so far.

At forty minutes I've become stiff and sore from the strain of the ropes and from my harness digging into me. It's so easy to become despondent or complacent when you're tired. It's simpler not to think, not to keep with the present, and to allow the mind to wander. I clench my teeth. Resignation and idle thoughts are not going to get me out of here. Only experience can pull me through.

In 1998 I'd written to the British Special Forces. I had ended up as part of the first group of women to undergo a rigorous selection course. Had I known how gruelling the course was, I would not have had the courage or self-belief to sign up. It was only sheer determination and encouragement from some of the training staff and other candidates that enabled me to push through it.

For nearly a year I'd endured long periods of demanding exercise regimes, coupled with living in muddy dugout shelters or under a sheet of plastic. I never knew what to expect, and the familiarity of uncertainty became a certainty in itself. We learned how to rely on each other and how to cope with fear. It was an unforgettable experience, and the greatest amount of effort I had ever put into one single thing. At the end of our nine months of training the colonel came to congratulate us. We were told we had set a benchmark as the first women ever to go through this training, and should be proud of our efforts.

What left a deeper impression was something I could not see or quantify. They call it grit. It's the ability to endure hardship for extended periods of time. Applied to a more urban environment it's that quality that enables people to persevere relentlessly until a problem is resolved, or to push through in order to meet a series of demanding deadlines.

Now, here we are in comparable circumstances, deprived of basic needs like sleep, warmth and food, where every minute is uncertain. I will need every ounce of grit to keep going.

I purse my lips. What would our corporal or colonel say now? I can see the others – Dex and the horrible tall, skinny one whose name I could never remember. What would they think of me gibbering on the end of a rope? They'd tell me to 'get with it', 'pull yourself together', to 'keep going'.

So I knock my feet against the vertical wall and bang my hands so the frostbite can't eat further into my skin. I pull back the cuffs of my waterproof and blow on my wrists to keep the circulation going.

"Come on, girl. Come on." I'm not going to give up. Whatever happens I'm not giving up.

As I blow on my wrist I look up. My torch catches a glint of metal, something not completely hidden by snow. It's a few metres above me.

I study its outline. It's irregular and sharp, protruding horizontally from the rock. It's a metal piton hammered into the rock many years back. I search through snapshot memories of our climb. It seems like an awfully long time ago.

Perhaps it's the corporal's goading voice in my mind that taunts me to look up again.

I can't climb high enough to scrape away the ice to see what lies beneath, so I decide to use the beam from my torch. Carefully I remove the torch from the helmet and hold it close to the cliff, beam shining up. Any pegs, even if covered with snow, will cast a shadow where they protrude from the rock. As I wave the light across the face, silvery stalactites of ice dance in the light.

It's difficult to see clearly because every minute or so more snow tumbles down the cliff, blowing spindrift into my eyes. I work the torchlight across the area where the pitons should be, moving the beam upwards, along, then up again and horizontally across. I've nearly given up when, just out of sight, I see a hook shape covered in frost. I move the light back and there's another lump. I can't be sure the lump isn't just a protrusion of rock. I stare a very long time at the face. Eventually I'm certain.

I've worked out where we are. In my mind I'm able to trace back the sequence of moves from the difficult section above to our belay stance, then back along the awkward traversing section that precedes it. I estimate we're about twenty metres short of the next station, where there's a small ledge and a couple of bolts. It's flanked out of sight to my left.

Despite our best efforts to remain on the ridge with our abseils, the ropes are running right over the side of it. We're still very high on the ridgeline, and either side the mountain is flanked by glaciers. Even if we were to survive the series of abseils straight down the side, we'd eventually land in the deeply-crevassed Cengalo glacier.

The wind whistles and howls and ice keeps stinging my cheeks. For protection I cover my face with my hands. I think of Jeremy exposed to the storm on the other end of the rope. I imagine he will search in the line of fall, and then pull the ropes sideways trying to locate the next rap station. This could loosen boulders above him. It makes me feel sick with guilt. It had been my suggestion to go straight down.

I wait and wait and wait.

I'm sure soon enough he'll realise my route suggestion is incorrect. That he'll be jumaring back up the lines to try another approach. Or so I think. Then I can show him what I've found, and thereby correct our path.

Ten minutes of waiting goes by. Another ten. It's been an hour and still there's no sign of Jeremy. I estimate how long it will have taken him to get down, how much time he may have spent searching for the next abseil station before realising things aren't right. How long will it take him to jumar back up the ropes? Surely it can't have taken over an hour?

Snow and hail pelt down, great forks of lightning flash and thunder blasts. I've stopped being scared of the lightning. It's out of my control. I stamp my feet and bang my hands to prevent them freezing further. Every so often I curl up to protect myself from the cold.

I know something must be up.

I feel trapped. Jeremy's bodyweight is keeping the ropes firmly anchored, and I'm tied to the other end. It's not possible to abseil down to him with his weight still holding the ropes taught. I look at my watch again. Surely by now if he'd realised it wasn't the right direction, he'd have come back up the lines to me?

Okay, fifteen minutes, and then you can worry, I think.

But I know if I think about things too much, I'll become completely unnerved. Singing seems a good way of taking my mind off things. I settle on 'Born Free'.

Hearing my own voice is an odd consolation. It reminds me I'm alive. As I sing, memories of Africa, home and all the places and people I love flood my mind. For a little while it removes thoughts of the cold storm and I feel comforted.

Then I look up and say a little prayer. I don't want to say too much because I think I might cry. Other than just being alive, I try hard to think of something to be thankful for. As I study the patterns of snow spinning in the storm, the ice crystals and the purple-pink lightning, it becomes very beautiful. Most people can only ever dream of hanging from a cliff in the middle of the night and seeing such a spectacle. And here I am in the middle of it. It is an incredible privilege and if it's to be the last sight I ever have, then I appreciate it for its power and beauty.

An hour and a half has passed. It's all a living nightmare. I think about what might have happened to Jeremy, about what action needs to be taken. Sometimes there are a myriad of possibilities and outcomes, but if you can narrow down the selection to three or four, then it's easier to find a solution.

I decide to wait another fifteen minutes. After that I'll edge down on prussicks and deal with whatever has to be dealt with. I try lifting the ropes to see if there's been any movement. They're still taut. I cry at my weakness, at the situation, at hanging deserted in space. I reach into my rucksack for the spare prussick cord and place it in my pocket ready for use.

Fifteen minutes can become a void, where each second takes an age to pass. I stare at my watch willing the minutes on. I set myself the challenge of only looking at it again at five-minute intervals. In between, I determine, I'll occupy the time with positive thoughts. I tell myself there are only two things on which to concentrate – Jeremy's life and my own.

Twelve minutes pass. Three minutes to go. I begin to wind the first prussick onto the ropes. Then I pull out the piece of cord from my pocket so I can lever my weight from one cord clasp to the next, and inch my way down. I try hard to focus on what I'm doing. Not to think about what I might see. My body is shaking inside. I have to take deep breaths, to think of this as a job.

The lightning flashes. I shut out all fearful thoughts and concentrate on attaching everything correctly. If this is my time to go, then I'll go trying. Again the golden light, now directly below and brighter, flashes up the face. My heart thumps. Adrenaline surges through my body. I feel like jelly. I lean right back in my harness and peer over the edge.

Snowflakes dance in a yellow beam of light. The 'lightning' had been Jeremy's head torch flashing upwards as he checked how much further he still had to go. I blink, and look again. Had I not been so frightened and exhausted, I'd be laughing at my error. Jeremy pushes his jumars up the lines and hauls up. I reach out to help him over the last step. His body is soaked in perspiration. He's exhausted.

But he's beside me, clipped in, his arms wrapped round me. For a moment I forget we're hanging over a precipice. I bury my head into his chest, relieved. His heart beats loudly. His body is warm and wet. I want to say something, but nothing comes out. I point to the row of pitons above us to show him where we are.

Jeremy pads sideways across the face. If he lowers himself too far it will be difficult for him to regain the crest. The ropes are at an acute angle by the time he reaches the end. He lunges for the edge. He hauls over and disappears from sight.

I know it will be a hard act to follow. After a few minutes the ropes slacken. I prepare to move. I feel apprehensive at the prospect of swinging across the face. What if something goes wrong? But I'm relieved to be moving from the place where I've been hanging for two hours. I lean back and slowly allow some of the rope to feed through until I reach the lip of the overhang. I start inching across the ice, first one foot and then the other. I push further across. I need to let out just a little more slack, to take another couple of steps sideways and I'll be there. As the line swings through vertical and I move upwards, I push hard with my legs to get further across. I'm almost there. Just a little further. I lunge forward to give extra momentum to the last little bit. My feet slip. I scrabble against the ice, swing through space unable to see where I'll land. My right hand hits something hard in the dark. My hand goes limp, followed by a horrible deep ache.

I stop swinging and stamp my foot against the face in frustration. I'm angry. It's that kind of detached 'cool' aggression where determination controls anger and anger becomes power. I lose any fear of the pitons sliding out, or the ropes tearing over the roof. I push hard with my legs, then race back along the face and back towards the edge. With every ounce of strength I throw myself in a giant leap at the end of the pendulum to catch the flake of rock.

As I leap I let go of the ropes and keep staring at the point I'm aiming for. My hands hit the rock. I grasp tight. For a moment I forget the burning pain in my hand and cling to the outcrop. Quickly, I scrabble my feet against the cliff below and haul my body up and over the edge. My head pitches forward and I roll over, landing in a rather ungraceful bundle of legs and arms on a tiny, flat ledge the size of a coffee table.

8 The first night

Battling the wind and snow for hours has left us exhausted. We're standing huddled together on the only sheltered place on the entire one and a half kilometre ridgeline. The ledge is just over a metre and a half long and half a metre wide, with a gravestone-size boulder in front and a wall of frozen rock behind. To our left and right is a drop of about a thousand metres into the crevasses below.

After a series of close shaves, lightning is still charging our head torches, and we're reluctant to push our luck further in the dark. I'm especially relieved because my hand is sore and I'm not sure how much control I'd have guiding the ropes through the abseil device. Even if nothing else happens, it's becoming impossible to stand up in the gale-force winds, and once we leave the partial shelter of the rock ledge we know we'll probably be swept off the ridgeline.

We've been climbing almost twenty hours and, in that time, have eaten only one proper meal – just before setting off. Our liquid carbohydrate drinks are frozen inside their containers.

Jeremy scrapes the ice from a crack in the frozen wall behind us. He wiggles in some pieces of metal equipment, and attaches our nylon slings, now hard with ice. The loose end is clipped onto the front loop of our harnesses to stop us from accidentally tripping or being blown off the ledge.

We take it in turns to scrape away the snow at our feet to create a small hole to sit in. While Jeremy digs, I bang my hands together. Then we swap places. I use my good hand to dig, the other as a kind of scoop to

On Table Mountain, Cape Town, South Africa

Leading at Castle Rock, Cumbria, UK

Practising aid climbing before an expedition to climb the North Face of Half Dome in Yosemite, USA

Deep water solo climbing above the sea in Swanage, UK
Inset: Sport climbing in the Cederberg, South Africa

Climbing in the Wye Valley, Wales
(left and right)

Enjoying a route in the French Alps

Walking up to climb a route in Scotland

Jeremy and me in the French Alps, Mont Blanc Massif

Left: Jeremy coiling ropes in the Swiss Alps
Right: Jeremy in the French Alps

Abseiling in to attempt a new icefall climb in Norway

Leading a tricky pitch in the Alps

Climbing the northeast face of the Eiger

Hours after our ordeal, with Piz Badile in the background, top right.

Safe and sound, and engaged, back in London.

excavate areas which have loosened. The snow is frozen solid onto the rocks below, and we manage to carve out just a shallow hollow. We build up the sides a little. It provides a tiny bit of extra shelter.

Jeremy suggests we de-ice the ropes by running our gloved hands down them, then coil them into the black dustbin bags with which we had lined our rucksacks. This will prepare our ropes for the next abseil in the morning, by which time we hope the storm will have passed. We sit on the dustbin bags, a small barrier between ourselves and the icy hollow beneath and us.

Being inactive, our bodies rapidly start to cool. The combination of a low ambient temperature and gale-force winds has created a windchill effect far below the actual temperature. With snow falling over a kilometre and a half below our bivi platform, nearly three thousand metres up, the temperature has dipped below –10 °C.

We pull out our emergency shelter. These shelters are made from a light fabric that is windproof and breathable. They pack into a tiny stuff sac and can be carried in the bottom of even the smallest of rucksacks. The only downside is that the sizing allocated by manufacturers is not too generous. Our shelter was designed for two people. Jeremy and I are both light and small-framed, and had practised crawling inside our shelter during one of our planning sessions. Perched on a mountain in a howling gale, the shelter seems much smaller as we squeeze into it, but the cocoon of fabric makes an instant difference. It blocks out the worst of the wind. Our breath and body heat keep things from instantly freezing.

But there's always a downside to comfort. Now that we're sitting in one place and not moving, we're more likely to get frostbite. As the body becomes colder it reduces circulation to the extremities, so that its energy can be used to supply blood to the vital organs. Numbness in the fingers and toes is the first symptom of this process. The tiny capillaries constrict, restricting blood flow, and slowly the cells freeze. Once the cells have been frozen for some time, they become white and wooden. At this point there is general tissue damage, known as 'frostnip' – the tissue is unlikely ever to recover fully. If these damaged areas are re-exposed to cold later in life, the shutting down process is far more rapid, and frostbite can happen very quickly.

Frostbite is more severe than frostnip. With frostbite the exposed cells die. The white tissue first turns dark purple, then black. The black area is like a dead piece of bark. Gradually it separates from the healthy or partially damaged tissue around it and falls off or, in extreme cases, becomes septic and rots.

My career relies on my having a full complement of toes and fingers, and a healthy physique. Losing parts of my body to frostbite is not an option.

I suggest we create a system for checking our fingers and toes, making sure they haven't become frostbitten. The only way we can do this, is to visually check our hands and feet at regular intervals, and to find a means of keeping them from freezing solid. We're too cold to warm our feet by placing them under each others' arms, or between our legs. I've been told you should not rub or bang frostbitten areas, but I can't think of any other way to bring back the circulation. We set up a rotation to warm fingers and toes every hour. Weather permitting, we'll set aside fifteen minutes for this task, every hour on the hour. In-between, we'll spend a certain amount of time sorting out and maintaining our equipment and the shelter, and then we'll have fifteen minutes of 'free' time to relax. In comparison to our very active day-to-day living, this will be an enforced 'rest'.

We begin our first round of checking almost immediately. Jeremy and I snuggle up to gain as much heat as possible from our bodies – sitting opposite each other, our legs entwined. I probably have the advantage, as Jeremy's body naturally emits more heat.

To prevent the survival shelter tearing by moving about too much, we work on each other's feet by unfastening one shoe at a time and working our way round the foot. We rub and bang the white areas until they turn pink again. It's fairly excruciating to have someone else rub your feet to restore circulation. As the feet begin to regain sensitivity they burn with a deep, aching pain. It's so uncomfortable I want to kick out. I have to exert tremendous self-control to go against my instincts and keep still. If we rip our shelter, we'll destroy our barrier from the storm.

Once we complete the foot-rubbing task we take a hard-earned break. It's important for us to find things to be positive about, and to reward each small achievement, even if it's just rewarding the completion of a basic task, or congratulating ourselves on working together effectively, or in finding the best way to shelter from the wind. Our reward at this stage is to sit back and take a mental and physical break from trying to survive.

However, we know that even during our 'down' time we have to maintain a level of vigilance and self-discipline. If we just lie back and relax, hypothermia will creep up on us.

Hypothermia occurs when the body cools to the point where it slowly shuts down. The visual symptoms of hypothermia are obvious: lips turning bluish, discoloration of the fingers, shivering ...

Mentally, people go through various hypothermic stages, from hyperactivity and deliriousness, to becoming sluggish, lethargic, and confused. Hypothermia happens in different ways and at varying speeds. It doesn't always require subzero temperatures. It can also be triggered by windchill, exhaustion, and lack of food.

For us the warning bells will be fatigue and an almost uncontrollable desire to go to sleep. In the army, or on a boat, it's often possible to set up a roster so one person can sleep while the others keep watch. Here, we're just a team of two, isolated and exhausted by intense activity and cold. If we take turns to sleep, it will be too tempting for the other to close their eyes for five minutes and then not wake up. We choose to stay awake. Even though we know this might be for a very long time, with both of us awake we'll be able to encourage the other to keep at it.

During our first rest period we discuss strategies to keep ourselves awake during the long night ahead. Our 'duties' will depend on the wind, as every now and again it blows in a huge gust and we need all our energy to keep the shelter from blowing away.

And so it happens during one of our 'rest' periods that we lean against my rucksack. We hear a strange, high-pitched 'beep' over the noise of the wind. It sounds like a mobile phone being switched on. I remember, now, that the mobile phone was the last item I'd squeezed into the bag. I wriggle around trying to find it. After a few minutes of shifting legs and wriggling my bottom off the rucksack without tearing or losing the shelter, the phone is in my hands.

Now comes the big moment. The phone is showing just two bars of battery, which will deplete quickly due to the cold. We need to decide what we're going to do, and to do it fairly smartly.

Astonishingly, the phone has three bars of reception. Will we be able to send a message for help?

It may seem strange we don't immediately dial the rescue number, but at this stage we don't know whether we needed rescuing. Many climbers land in situations from which they perform self-rescues, and most people would see this as the first option.

Apart from my swollen wrist neither of us is seriously injured. We're just cold, hungry, tired and in the dark. We're pretty sure we can sit out the night, and if the weather abates we'll be able continue our abseil the following morning.

The only real problem is that the predicted mild conditions have transformed into a stormy blizzard.

Although our clothing and equipment are geared for a lightweight, technically-difficult rock-climbing ascent, we had prepared ourselves with some emergency equipment many would probably not carry – our shelter, and an extra layer of thermal clothes. But since the storm blew in, we know that continuing our descent without ice axes, crampons, and heavy-duty winter clothing would be foolhardy. If the weather persists it will be impossible to abseil off the ridge without being blown over. The wind is now gusting at around a hundred and thirty kilometres an hour. It will be impossible to negotiate abseiling down a tricky ridgeline covered in ice and snow, even with rigid mountaineering boots and crampons. Thick snow will have obliterated any trace of the fixed anchors or rocky crevices from which to set up belays.

This ledge is the only sheltered area that we can recall. Once we set off from where we are, there'll be no way of retracing our footsteps, and no option of stopping. It will take just a few hours before we'll be suffering from severe hypothermia or frostbite. I know I've already lost a significant amount of dexterity in my right hand from banging it on our last abseil. To start out in a less than good physical condition will compromise us further.

We decide to give ourselves an hour to think things through. We'll then do our foot and hand rubbing, and act on our decision.

In the end it's fairly simple. There are two choices: raise the alarm for rescue now, or wait until morning and then review the situation.

By waiting till the morning we'll not feel we're throwing in the towel on a situation that might improve. Against this, though, is the possibility the storm will continue longer than expected, perhaps even for a week. It is better to inform rescue workers while we're still in a fit condition to do so. That way they'll be able to make a plan to get to us. Even this might take a while – particularly if the bad weather persists.

Despite our location and the severe weather, when I check the phone we still have a signal. It's only reading three bars, but it will probably work. There is no guarantee we'll have a signal later, or that the battery will survive in the cold. It seems pretty obvious we should grab the opportunity while it's within our grasp. Once the call has been made, all we'll have to do is concentrate on surviving the night. As long as our shelter remains intact this is possible. With the decision made I feel relieved.

The battery has limited life and we know our call has to be precise, short and correct first-time. We dial the number for Swiss rescue and wait. An automated response comes up in what sounds like Swiss-German. The call is rejected. For some reason my phone is unable to put the call through. They require some sort of code. I had enquired about this before we set off from London, and had been told there would be no problem.

I try again. The same thing happens. Jeremy suggests we dial an English rescue number, but that doesn't work either.

Here we are, having survived all the dangers and obstacles en route, only to be stopped by this technological hurdle. Frustration gives way to despair.

9 Making the A-list

Our greatest glory is not in never falling but in rising every time we fall.
CONFUCIUS

To continue dialling the number and getting the same response will just waste airtime and battery power. As we sit in the shelter, Jeremy and I decide the last option will be to try and text some of our friends back in England. Together we compose a short message. We decide to send the message to five of our most reliable friends. It feels weird writing a message asking for help – it's not something I thought I'd ever have to do. We don't want to alarm people, but at the same time we need to send them as much information as concisely as possible – an indication of the seriousness of the situation. We're concerned that if we write something like, 'Help, we need rescuing' people might think it a practical joke.

It will waste too much battery life to try to turn off the predictive texting, so I break down each of the unrecognisable words into short sections, separated by a space: 'Need heli rescue. north ridge Piz Bad ile, Swit zer land.'

Once we've prepared our text message, we move through my phone directory to find five friends who'll take our call for help seriously. We make an A-list and, in case no one responds after the first message, a B-list.

The people in our A-list include my friend Ruth. We are set to go on an expedition to Tibet in the next three weeks, and had originally planned to go shopping for thermal underwear this weekend. She's a PA to a director of a large financial institution, and is unflappable and quick-thinking.

We also send a message to my friend Tim, who led our team of four on the Borneo Eco Challenge some years earlier. He is ex-military, and I think he'll certainly take our message seriously.

I have a Swiss-Italian friend, Seba. I'd spent time training him and his friends for a technical rock climb in Wadi Rum. I thought he might know the area we're in because he and his father had used a local Italian mountain guide and had climbed extensively in the region.

Then Richard – my ex-boyfriend. I'm a little reluctant to send the message to him as I think he might worry. However, he is the brainiest person I know, and will go as far as getting diplomats and politicians involved to get us out should it come to that. I also know he'll probably contact another friend, Phil, who has climbed the route we're on, and knows the area well.

Finally, Avery. Avery is the American photojournalist with whom I'd been ice climbing in Italy the previous year. He is an experienced climber with a wicked sense of humour. We'd become good friends since meeting at a climbing wall a couple of years back. Just before starting up the first climb, he'd stopped me, held out the belay apparatus in his hand and, in his mid-western drawl, asked, "So wad are these for?" My eyes widened in disbelief. He chuckled loudly. "Oh man, I had you there."

We became firm friends and I discovered Avery to be someone who would go to great lengths to accomplish things.

I tell Jeremy I have a feeling that if anyone can do anything, it will be Avery. He has a way of making people listen to him, of not just accepting things when they don't go his way. I tell Jeremy if things don't work out, Avery will probably kick up a big fuss and get international news broadcasters involved.

The friends we select are all based in England. I don't want to contact anyone in South Africa in case the news finds its way back to my parents. They can do without knowing we're stuck on a mountain.

We press 'send', and wait.

It seems like ages before the 'message sent' sign comes up. Now all we can do is wait. We switch off the phone, and decide to turn it on again at eight the next morning. We want to wait as long as possible, thereby increasing the chance of a response, because it would be pretty disheartening to switch on the phone and find no replies.

It is one o' clock in the morning. My friends, who are not great party animals, are likely to be sound asleep.

To save its battery life, Jeremy puts the phone inside his jacket – the warmest place for it. Then it's time to rub feet and hands again. Once more we set about the task of banging and rubbing until circulation returns.

We've been in the shelter only a couple of hours and already our bodies are cramped and stiff. The night seems endless. Snow is falling heavily and we keep patting it off the top of the shelter.

Every now and again we hear an eerie whining. It starts off far away, gaining in volume as it approaches. We soon learn what it is. As the wind travels up from the crevasses, it moans and howls until it reaches us. At this stage, we grasp the shelter as tightly as we can to prevent it blowing away. It's like tug o' war with an invisible giant. As hard as we pull down, so the wind tries to rip the shelter from our grasp. The blue nylon billows out like a spinnaker, then snaps back into our faces, smothering us and making a 'bub-bub-bub' sound as it sticks to us. Intermittently, flashes of lightning light up the dark space turning everything an eerie pink. The lightning is accompanied by thunder booming in the night sky around us. Being in the shelter, squashed in the crevice between the rocks, I feel less afraid of the lightning than when we'd been abseiling down the ridgeline.

Jeremy becomes very cold and starts to shiver. He has used a lot of energy jumaring those fifty metres back up the ropes after I'd sent him down the wrong way. The perspiration had nowhere to go. His underlayers of clothing became soaked, and now lie cold and wet against his skin. I worry because he doesn't normally feel the cold as much as I do.

Throughout the night we think of different strategies to keep ourselves motivated and warm. To begin with, we try something I learned from my military training. One of the tasks my group of three was given was to dig a secret shelter and to keep watch from this shelter for a few days at a time. We had limited time to dig the shelter and disguise it with vegetation. My digging skills are not fantastic, which meant our shelter was cramped. When we swapped duties, we had to roll over each other in the mud and the dark. It was raining, with water leaking in through the entrance hole, making our manoeuvres a real mud bath. To wriggle about in such a confined space, we had to communicate in detail each movement we were about to perform, and to maintain a cool head when we ended up cramped and squashed in a dark, tight spot, with our noses pressed against the mud roof.

Our manoeuvring on the ledge is pretty similar except, thankfully, Jeremy is more flexible and lighter than most men. We change positions to use our combined body heat to greater effect. The move is performed within the emergency shelter, to maintain the heat that has already been generated. It proves to be an excellent way to while away a good fifteen or twenty minutes, to warm up, and to take our minds off the wait. Jeremy's quite good at twisting and swivelling, and I probably squash him more than he does me. We're tied in and occasionally have to unclip to avoid becoming tangled in the slings. There are a few awkward moments when we get tangled up. It's so bizarre we have to laugh.

Our next position is for Jeremy to sit behind me with his legs wrapped round me. This gives me more protection from the elements. After a while we swap around so Jeremy is able to take a break from having his back against the wind and his legs stuck against the frozen rock.

Once again it's time to rub hands and feet. We switch on our torches and perform the task. Having our torches on is another of our rewards – we need to keep the batteries going for as long as possible. When we switch off we make a conscious decision to remain awake, because naturally we've been brought up to associate darkness with sleep.

One of the best ways in which to stay awake is to keep talking. I'm pretty good at talking. In a tight spot it's always easy to remember stories about other people's misfortunes. The worse their misfortune, and the greater their triumph over adversity, the better. It places one's own problems into perspective.

One of the stories we recall is an old South African tale about a little girl called Rachel de Beer, and her younger brother. They'd been caught in an unexpected snowstorm on the highveld, where it only snows once in every twenty years or so. The only shelter was a large anthill that had been hollowed out to create a kind of oven for baking bread. They crawled into the anthill, and little Rachel sat at the entrance to block off the cold air. She also took off her clothes and gave them to her younger brother to keep him warm. When the two children were eventually found, Rachel was no longer alive, but because of her bravery her brother had survived.

We try to think of jokes, but the only funny thing that pops into my mind are the words of some great explorer who suggested one should choose a team wisely, because you may have to eat them.

This probably would have been more amusing were we not so hungry, and thirsty. We've tried defrosting our emergency liquid carbohydrate drinks under our arms and in our groin areas, but our bodies are too cold to melt anything. Our stomachs have gone through numerous rumbling and aching-hunger stages, followed by short bouts of nausea from lack of food. The rumbles usually last a brief period, and afterwards the hunger subsides a while. We realise the less we focus on it, the less hungry we'll feel. But this particular rumble is lasting a long time.

Then I remember something.

"Jeremy, do you still have that packet of peanuts?"

Jeremy reaches into his jacket and produces the blue packet.

We have our new motivation-survival kit right in our hands. It's now 3 a.m., and the seriousness of our situation is sinking in. We don't know how long we'll be on this ledge, or if anyone has received our messages.

The storm seems to be intensifying, which means we could be stuck for days. There's a limit as to how long we can stay alive, shivering in the cold, without a stove, water or full survival kit. We create our own rota of duties, relaxation and reward because, in reality, the situation is a never-ending monotony of misery that can easily lead to despair.

We decide to eat two peanuts each every four hours. It's a reward for surviving that little bit longer. I'm in charge of the peanuts. Jeremy looks after the mobile phone. We eat the first two just after 3 a.m. We know that at 7 a.m. we'll be able to eat two more. It takes a great deal of willpower not to gobble them all down. I try to make the experience last longer by swirling each one round in my mouth. Knowing we're both undergoing the same experience makes it easier for us to stick to our plan – something that is particularly difficult with churning, grumbling stomachs. Sharing this experience with Jeremy, and seeing how he copes inspires me to keep going.

It's soon time to readjust our positions again – my turn to be on the inside – before settling down to our foot and hand maintenance. Between times the wind buffets against the shelter and we're forced to hold it down and curl up as tightly as we can to protect ourselves. I switch on my torch and check the time: 4 a.m. Only two hours till dawn. That's one hundred and twenty minutes. Every minute being sixty seconds long, just long enough to exchange a greeting, or to hold one's breath without turning blue. Sixty seconds is very short, I tell myself. I'm able to cope with the idea of one hundred and twenty of these short periods of time. In fact, just that thought has already reduced the total to a hundred and eighteen.

10 The second day

When friendships are real, they are not glass threads, or frostwork,
but the solidest things we know.
RALPH WALDO EMERSON

Throughout the night our survival shelter billows out, then snaps back
in our faces. We try to limit the amount of air curling underneath,
but somehow drafts manage to find their way in. As the air surges up
between the cracks, it blows the sheet out like a full spinnaker. We switch
on our torches and stare at the taut seams, wondering how long it will be
before they rip apart. Then the wind reverses direction, the shelter snaps
back. We're showered with ice crystals that have formed from frozen
condensation on the roof. A fresh gust then hurls the snow in another
direction, and the whole process starts again.

All through the night we battle, with Jeremy shouting, "Hold tight,"
each time a new gust tears at us. I grip the spare ends of the shelter,
driven by the terrifying thought of the sheet being torn from my grasp
and blowing away. I picture it hooking over some icy, out-of-reach
pinnacle. If left exposed we will start to freeze within minutes.

It's like being locked in a home freezer – icy and claustrophobic. We
have to control and plan each of our movements if we're to prevent the
shelter from tearing. The muscles in my back and legs are cramping
from the cold and dehydration. Each time a spasm sears through me I
scrunch my eyes and bite my lips. I pray for the self-discipline to not to
shout out or writhe in agony. I keep hoping I won't have to stay in this
position too much longer. I try to think of something to take my mind
off the pain and the desperate need to straighten my body. We have to

work together to survive this, and this means not complaining. I'm sure Jeremy feels similar discomfort.

6 A.M.

Overnight our bodies have cooled. We're weak from lack of food and sleep. Although we'd planned to wait until 8 a.m. to check for a reply on our phone, by 6 a.m. we can't hold out any longer. We switch on the phone and sit impatiently. It's a race between time and a fading battery life.

For a moment the phone hovers around three bars, then drops to two. The little graphic 'Welcome' motif flicks up on the screen. Endless time passes.

'Beep beep' ... The signal comes up.

It's a message from Avery. Quickly I open it, breathing deeply.

'Am on the case.'

Both of us sit back for a moment, relieved and exhausted. Then I start worrying.

Has he misinterpreted our message? Is he responding to a text from someone else?

Our texts have to be short and clear, requesting or delivering only essential information. Normally emergency police numbers are free and operate regardless of international cell phone restrictions. We figure it will be the best number to use should we lose contact with Avery. We write our reply, and press the 'send' button.

'Please call Swiss air rescue. Text reply and Swiss police number.'

Finally 'message sent' flashes up and we can relax for a while.

Avery sends the number for the police, and asks our exact location. We switch off our phone and think exactly how to describe where we are. We're fortunate that on this thousand metre ridgeline, we happen to be at a feature mentioned in the route description from the guidebook.

'Red Arrow area about three hundred metres below the summit north ridge, Piz Badile. On route. Behind detached rock. Blue shelter.'

We send Avery an additional text saying we'll switch on our phone every four hours to check for new messages.

The lightning and thunder continue, but by now we're accustomed to it. We set about sticking to our routine.

7 A.M.

At 7 a.m. we have 'breakfast' – two peanuts each. The time between is spent rubbing feet, hands and doing a position swap. There is a slight lull in the wind. I crawl from the shelter to have a pee. It's the first time I'm able to catch a glimpse of where we are by daylight. The view makes me feel ill. Sometimes at night things are intimidating because your vision is limited by darkness. Seldom is it actually worse in daylight.

I take half a step from the shelter and reach the precipice. Some snow falls over the edge. Between the clouds, a vertical drop plummets hundreds of metres. In a few seconds the swirls of snow and spindrift turn everything white again. It's horribly disorientating.

There's no room for modesty up here. As I squat over the edge I remove a glove so I can loosen my overtrousers and draw the flap of my long johns to one side. I'd never realised how useful my sale long johns would be. They are a rather progressive design with a vertical split from the waistband at the front to the waistband at the back. For modesty an extra layer of material flapped over, which can be drawn to one side when needed. The idea is that women no longer need to take off their climbing harnesses or expose their entire midriffs and rears to the elements. I wish I'd bought more when they were on sale. (Sadly, the design was unpopular and was taken off the market the following season.)

Within thirty seconds, my ungloved hand turns white. It's like a piece of dead wood. Hastily I pull up my trousers and crawl back under the shelter. I rub, blow on, and stuff my fingers into my mouth to bring them back to life.

10 A.M.

When we switch on the phone two envelopes appear. I open the first. It's from Ruth.

'You're joking. Are we still going shopping for thermal underwear today, Rachel?'

We have to laugh. I want to write back, tell her where we are, how help is on the way. I even want to tell her about my handy long johns. Ruth has a great sense of humour, but I'd never imagined her humour would travel so far, or into such a desperate situation. If we could have had any another person on our ledge, it probably would have been Ruth. She's able to make life seem funny even when it isn't.

But we choose to ignore all messages unless they are from Avery. This will avoid the confusion of trying to explain different things to different parties, and will also save battery life. I feel bad not responding to Ruth, as she'll be left wondering, but we can't think of something to tell her that won't cause her worry.

Avery asks if anyone has been injured, and how many of us are on the climb.

We're finding it difficult to concentrate, so we each check our responses. With each message perhaps being the last to get through, we can't afford a mistake.

Back in London Avery is waiting by his phone. It's around 11 a.m.

Avery

I knew things were not looking too good, and there was little I could do except send and relay messages to help the rescue operation. A message flashed up and I opened it. It read, 'Onl injured. Two. Heavy row storm last night t star.'

This should have answered some of the questions I'd sent, but the reply made no sense at all. I became concerned. It was the writing of someone mentally confused. This could be caused by hypothermia. Rachel had managed to press buttons and reply, but that was about it. It might already be too late. I picked up the phone and called air rescue again. I wanted to ask why they haven't been able to get to her yet. Surely putting a helicopter in the sky couldn't be that hard?

What the message should have read was, 'No one injured. Two of us. Heavy snow storm last night.'

On the ground the rescue teams are kicking their heels. They're all waiting and ready to fly, but the winds are so strong in the valley that the chopper is unable to lift off. They have tried. It's just too dangerous. If the winds were so violent in the valley, they can only imagine what the conditions are at three thousand metres. They wait. The pilot rechecks the wind-speed, its direction, and the pressure readings. He sits near the chopper, hoping the storm will die down. The forecast isn't promising. All they can do is hope.

Then Avery's phone rings. The BBC has heard that a young South African-born woman is in trouble in the Alps. News travels fast in the media world. Avery has anxiously confided in a friend and, in no time, reporters want to know whether the story is indeed true and, if so, has anyone attempted a rescue yet? The next call is from a news reporter. An American woman rings from CNN, hoping for live footage.

This is a unique story. It's the first time journalists have heard of someone texting from the top of a mountain halfway across the continent, asking for rescue. They're all keen for the scoop. The fact that the person is a woman adventurer who has recently been filmed for a television series about extraordinary people, simply adds to the story.

On the mountain the situation is worse. Every hour eats into our survival time. As our bodies cool, the frozen condensation that showers our bodies no longer melts. It remains frozen, and our waterproof jackets become hard.

Knowing rescue is on its way gives us motivation to hold out longer, not to give up. And mentally we feel able to keep going. This outlook, however, doesn't halt the laws of physics. As our clothing starts to freeze, we know it's fast becoming too late for rescue.

12 NOON

By midday Jeremy's bottom is numb. He's had his back to the wind, protecting me from the cold.

We hadn't known each other that well before this climb, but very quickly barriers have broken down. Politely I offer to check for frostbite, but I can't quite bring myself to rub the frozen bit. Instead I suggest we swap places.

We're parched. My head is thumping from the effects of dehydration, the thumping further enhanced by our being at three thousand metres. I reach under my waterproof for the bottle. It's still frozen. Our bodies have cooled so much overnight the carbohydrate drinks haven't defrosted. Perhaps some will defrost in my mouth. I'm desperate. Nothing flows from the bottle and my tongue just becomes ice cold.

It's time for another two peanuts, another round of foot rubbing. We remove our gloves and stuff them inside our jackets. Our toes have become glassy. It takes a lot of vigorous rubbing and slapping to start the circulation again. It's about five minutes before the blood starts to ooze back into the feet. The pain is so intense I want to cry. I think what it would be like to have my toes go black and drop off. Vanity alone keeps me at it – until my feet burn.

Our bodies cool further as the day wears on. Outer layers of clothing freeze, and become stiff like cardboard. Jeremy's feet are not doing too well. Now our plastic shopping bags, used as waterproof covering for our emergency clothes, come in handy. He uses them as a windproof layer between his feet and his mountain shoes. Seeing Jeremy with the plastic bags wrapped round his feet makes me very jealous – not a pleasant emotion. I hold back, accepting we need to share resources fairly. He has, after all, been sheltering me by wrapping himself around me. It's only fair he has the plastic bags.

We check for phone messages again, and are about to switch off when a new message comes through. It's from Rega, the Swiss organisation that aids people in distress in the Swiss Alps. We breathe a sigh of relief. They know where we are, and we're able to communicate directly. Even if no one can get to us, we begin to feel less isolated.

They ask whether any one is injured, how many are in the party. We keep our reply simple: 'No injuries, just cold.'

The rescuers realise we might attempt a self-rescue if they can't get to us. They also know, in these conditions, a self-rescue is hopeless.

Their next text reads, 'Stay where you are.'

Then we receive a text giving us an emergency number, and telling us to call them. The phone is answered by a man called Geri. He has a Swiss accent. It's comforting to speak to another human being, and difficult to keep the conversation to a minimum.

I tell him who we are, where we're calling from, how our battery power is low so I can't speak for long. He sounds calm and reassuring.

"Are you okay?" he asks.

"We're fine. Just a bit cold ... and quite hungry."

Perhaps it's foolish pride, or an unwillingness to face the truth, but I can't bring myself to tell him how awful things really are. It is general protocol among climbers to underestimate their situation. If I start to relay how cold we really are, that we're getting frostbite, that we're very, very hungry, I might start crying. It will just make the rescue team feel awful if they can't get to us. It's better for him just to have the basic facts and to work with those. He's sure to be a mountaineer himself, and will know the route and the predicament we face. We can't afford to waste the life of our phone on things that can't be changed.

Geri says a rescue attempt will be made when the wind has calmed a little. We say goodbye. I switch off the phone.

I'd been hoping the rescue team would scramble immediately, like they do in the films. With each passing minute my heart sinks more as I realise the film-style rescue is not going to happen.

Later we receive another message. 'Wind too strong to fly. Geri.'

I feel angry and upset, but there's little use wasting valuable energy on those emotions, or in dragging Jeremy down with me. We try to think of something positive.

What we don't know is that the weather has worsened in the valley as well. The rescue helicopter is snowed in because of the storm, and cannot take off until lunchtime. At 1.30 p.m. there's another message: 'Switch handy on when you hear chopper.'

We sit in anticipation, straining to hear an engine over the storm.

After forty minutes we think we detect a different sound. The noise grows and we're certain. We'll soon be out of here, our fear of freezing to death over. I brush aside feelings of apprehension about the storm, and look around to see if we need to pack anything. No, just the survival shelter. The ropes are already in plastic bags and can be carried as they are. The shelter will take only a few minutes to stuff back into its bag, something we'll be able to do while the rescuers set things up to airlift us off. I can almost feel that hot cup of tea in my hands.

When the chopper is close, we switch on the phone and crawl from the shelter into the wind. My face is immediately stung by a blast of ice particles. My whole body trembles. Although we've been extremely cold in our shelter, the weather outside is unbearable.

The helicopter moves alongside the mountain about fifty or so metres from the ridgeline, until it hovers just a little higher than us. I see the people inside. One of them is wearing a dark helmet. I jump up and down waving the bright blue shelter. The man wearing the dark helmet waves back. We have succeeded. I'm thrilled. Never have I experienced such relief.

The helicopter is very close now, the rotor blades 'wop, wop, wop' over the wind and the storm. It's a light craft with a sleek red design along its white body. It's experiencing difficulty hovering. The wind tosses it about like a small toy. When the pilot tries to manoeuvre it closer, there's even more turbulence. They back off.

The man waves again. I can see his face. Then the helicopter turns and flies away.

It looks like they're going for a second attempt. They circle, hover for a while, battling against the ferocious storm, then loop round and fly off. The craft becomes smaller and smaller until it's lost in the storm. The sound of the rotor blades fade. Finally all we hear is the wind. I'm dismayed. It's as if the whole thing's been a dream.

11 Another attempt

It is not the fittest, nor the most intelligent who survive,
but those who best adapt to change.
CHARLES DARWIN

We pull the shelter back over our heads, and resume our positions on the black bin liners. Jeremy pulls me into him, wraps his arms round me, and hugs me as he gently pulls my hair to one side and whispers in my ear.

"They know where we are. Now they're able to plan how to get us out. We have a chance. We just have to keep going."

His voice is calm and soothing. The small amount of heat transmitting from him is comforting.

Five years of serving in the South African Western Cape Mountain Rescue team means Jeremy has an inside knowledge of how rescue procedures work. Many people think a rescue operation is merely a case of dropping a line to pluck someone from an inaccessible place. It's seldom that easy, and although we haven't been saved on this first attempt, Jeremy is sure they will be back.

In the excitement I've forgotten to turn off the phone. It beeps in my pocket. Another text.

'Wind too strong to fly. Will try later. Geri.'

Geri's message confirms all we've been thinking. I feel better. I'm pleased there's a name at the end of the message. It makes me feel these are real people trying their utmost to get to us. If we give up, we'll not just be giving up on ourselves we'll be giving up on them, too.

It's almost time for 'lunch', although I don't use that word. We steer clear of topics such as food. It prevents us from dwelling on morbid thoughts. As I squeeze the packet to push out four more peanuts, I'm reminded of a story I was told by a former British soldier and prisoner of war.

His name is Fergus and he's a good friend of my aunt Angela. Angela had arranged for me to meet him one evening, but warned me I would need to set aside the whole evening, as Fergus would be keen to tell me about his life. He has a small flat with paintings and a poster of himself performing magic. Soon I found myself with a cup of tea in hand, listening to horrific scenes of war and inspiring tales of survival.

Fergus served in Burma, before being captured by the Japanese and being taken as a prisoner-of-war to build the bridge over the River Kwai. During this four-year period his only item of clothing was a loincloth he later kept in his top drawer as a souvenir of his survival. The prisoners had to rely on their ingenuity and resourcefulness to survive. Each day they were fed a small bowl of rice. Fergus told me how some would gobble theirs down very quickly, but that he would savour each grain by swirling it around in his mouth and deciding whether it was fatter and juicier than the last one.

As I tell Fergus's story to Jeremy, we practise his ritual with our peanuts, biting into each of the two peanuts separately, swirling them round in our mouths, tasting each little bit of salt and flavour.

The day drags on. We make a few adjustments to the shelter. Jeremy takes charge of all the 'housekeeping' duties, while I keep an eye on the timing of the 'administrative' tasks we've set ourselves.

I 'lodge a complaint' about a draft creeping through the cracks below. We need to sort this out. Jeremy scrapes mounds of snow from just outside the shelter and squashes it into the drafty holes. With the wind against it, the snow soon freezes. While not every windy gap can be sealed, he's made a big improvement. These are tiny accomplishments which, in our ordinary fast-paced life, would seem trivial. But we're working with a different currency now, and every little improvement is a triumph, worthy of recognition and reward.

Jeremy sets himself to re-racking the climbing equipment. It's a way of keeping mind and body occupied, of preventing him from falling asleep.

I'm too exhausted to join in, so I look on, trying to find something in the gear-racking process to hold my concentration. I'm not sure whether it's exhaustion or cold, but I'm struggling to motivate myself to perform active tasks that involve detailed thought processes.

Racking is a pretty simple job. It means sorting everything from smallest to largest, and placing like items with like. This is almost too complex for me to think about. It seems strange, because I've had no problem lucidly recalling stories about big events. It's easier for me to describe pictures in my mind, while for Jeremy it's easier to be involved in a physical, detailed task. We appear to be resorting to our 'base types' to help us survive.

The afternoon passes. The wind roars unabated. There's no sign of rescue. The Rega team and Avery send a few more messages. Finally, in the late afternoon, I suggest we should prepare for another night. I'm convinced it's not our time to die. There is nothing left to say. We shiver together in silence. It's at these low moments I keep saying, "Okay, I've a feeling we won't be rescued today, but I know we're going to get out of here. I know we'll be rescued. I know we'll live." I don't know why, I just know.

Jeremy, too, is positive, but his tendency is to rationalise.

4 P.M.

At around 4 p.m. Rega say they're about to attempt a second rescue. We're to be ready, to switch on the phone when we hear the sound of the rotor blades. They're waiting to the last possible moment before darkness in the hope the gale will die.

I try not to feel too hopeful. I keep telling Jeremy I'm sure they'll eventually get to us, but we shouldn't expect too much this afternoon. Whatever is happening in the valley hasn't changed where we are.

Our ears prick up each time there's a change in sounds around us then, just before dusk, we hear a distant hum, and the familiar 'wop, wop, wop' of a helicopter. Jeremy asks if I want to remain inside the shelter this time. I can't bear the idea of seeing the helicopter so close, then seeing it fly off again. I agree this is a good idea.

JEREMY

It was 5.30 p.m. by the time I crawled out of the shelter. The pilot attempted to manoeuvre the helicopter so that it hovered alongside us on the ridge. It succeeded briefly, but was soon buffeted by the wind. The small craft was again being tossed like a cork in the sea.

I signalled to the rescue team inside and they waved back. The helicopter made a big circle, then came round and tried to hover off the ridge again. I thought they might be looking for a flat place to lower somebody down. They tried, but couldn't get to us. I was disappointed – stranded once again. We were near enough to wave to one another, yet all the gesturing in the world wouldn't bring them closer. The reality was we were three kilometres up a mountain. They were fifty metres away, but in those sorts of conditions fifty metres are as good as five hundred kilometres.

There's no point standing in the cold any longer, and so Jeremy crawls back under shelter. Another message from Rega beeps through.

'Sorry Rachel, wind too strong, be strong, take care. Geri.'

We're on our own again. I want to cry. From the tone of the message they know the situation isn't good. Sometimes it's very hard to be strong. We'll have to wait until tomorrow and hope there's an improvement in the weather. We have to face another night on the mountain. Our bodies are now so cold we're shivering uncontrollably. We don't even know if physically we'll last that long.

Had the storm not been so violent, they might have had a minute or two to hover over the mountain to drop food, water and some dry clothes. But the risks were too great. They couldn't get any closer, nor had they been able to hover long enough in the same position. With sheer cliffs either side it had been impossible.

Perhaps we've been too brave. Perhaps, people need to know we aren't 'doing fine' – that every minute is a battle. We've tried to be as positive as possible, but now the time has come to let people know the truth of our deteriorating physical condition.

It's 8 p.m. and we send a message to Avery, 'If we're not rescued in the next twelve hours we stand little chance of survival.'

His reply is instant. 'They have seen you. They need weather to lift slightly. They will try in the morning.'

Both of us know Avery is being positive. He's telling the truth, but we know the weather will have to lift more than 'slightly' for anyone to get to us. Throughout the day he'd kept our spirits up by sending us cheery text messages and words of encouragement. I'm sure the 'what if' question has been playing in the backs of all our minds, but we'd chosen to ignore it.

There is an unpleasant 'what if' to every situation in life. On the whole, worrying about something you cannot change doesn't help. Sometimes, one's worst fears become reality and you're forced to confront the worst life has to offer.

I scroll down Avery's message. The end of it sends a shudder through my body. I read it to Jeremy.

'Shall I call someone for you?'

Both of us sit quietly, listening to the storm. I wonder whether other people who die from exposure and hypothermia in remote areas have gone through a similar process of realisation. Most of them wouldn't have been given an opportunity to say goodbye to their families. Even in this, the blackest moment imaginable, we're being offered an opportunity. Not the kind of opportunity I would hope for, but a chance for completion. I sit still. I'm dislocated from the truth. I keep asking, "Is this me? Is this really happening to me? I can't believe what is happening."

It is like watching a play and knowing how it ends. I could intervene with commentary, but it won't change the outcome.

Saying goodbye to those you love is not a decision taken lightly. It's even more difficult when that goodbye is said without sight, touch, or voice. I'm left wondering whether their pain and grief would be worse for the experience, or whether it would ultimately put their minds at peace. There is little life left in the phone. This might be our last occasion to use it.

12 The second night

The only way of finding the limits of the possible
is by going beyond them into the impossible.
ARTHUR C. CLARKE

We are utterly exhausted. I've been shivering non-stop for nearly two days. We've not had a sip of water, nor have we had any food except two peanuts every four hours. We've also been awake the entire time. I've only ever felt this weak once before whilst lying in hospital with a serious tropical disease – and then there had been medical staff monitoring developments on an hourly basis.

I read Avery's message again. I'm not sure whether we can stay awake any longer, whether we will even last till morning. I keep thinking, "This is really it. This is what happens before people die, and now it's happening to me."

It's as if the reality of our situation has come in waves, each wave rolling in with increasing seriousness. We can't escape. Abseiling through the storm had been difficult, but this is worse. It is relentless, and I can't see a way out. I had hoped one day to get married, to have a family. Now I'll be lucky to stay alive.

I think of those moments when I've been ungrateful and dissatisfied, even distraught, about some trivial matter. How I wish I could have any one of those moments back again. How differently I would live that experience now. I rub my gloved hands together, and whisper in the dark.

"Okay, Jeremy, what shall we do?" I try to sound brave, but my voice trembles, and seems to echo back.

We both know there is only one sensible option. We'll wait where we are, tempting though it is to think we might be able to abseil down. It doesn't take much to know we won't get very far before being swept off the cliffs, or before we freeze in the subzero temperatures.

More thoughts flood my brain ... 'farm school' under the trees outside our little thatched rondavel near the Magaliesberg mountains. Mum teaching me, Julian and the local sheep herder's children how to read with flashcards. The enjoyment of exciting family Christmases organised by Dad, building sandcastles at the seaside or going on safari. The adventures of farm life during the week – horse riding together, Mum sitting with us in the cool shade of the thatch, glasses of her homemade lemon juice at our elbows as she helps us with our homework. Then we'd rush out to play in the bright sunlight, returning hungry at sunset.

We grow older. Mum and Dad work long hours and are tired when they return from work each night. All that work to give us a good education, and all the other things we need.

My memory jolts forward. A long hospital corridor, my parents at one end, me approaching from the other. The sick feeling I have when I see the look on their faces, and Mum calling to me and saying, "Julian has gone. Rachel, Julian has gone." I feel so weak. My mind won't believe it ... I'll never see my brother again. He'd been in a car crash in Johannesburg, in the passenger seat. There'd been a collision with another car at an intersection. The driver and passenger in the back seat had been hospitalised. My brother had been cut from the wreckage and taken to intensive care.

My last memory of Julian was of us joking outside my student flat. He'd looked muscular, tanned, and healthy. We'd hugged goodbye, and as he drove off I'd reached to touch his arm through the open window. He'd cocked his head to one side and smiled. That is how I remember him.

"Jeremy, you know if we reply 'yes' to Avery, it will be like giving up. And our parents ..."

What will happen over the following days if we don't survive? I can't face the thought. The rescue team will find our bodies. From over ten thousand kilometres away someone will call my parents. The alternative is that Avery could phone them right now. He could send a last message from us telling them we love them. These are calls we can't make ourselves. Our phone doesn't work for international calls, and if we're serious about surviving, we'll need to use our phone battery wisely.

I can't. I just can't do that to my parents. I think of Avery. What a friend he is to offer to undertake such an unbearable task. While I know him well, he has never met my family, or that of Jeremy. How can I expect him to call them and break this news? What would be the benefit of him phoning our families? It will just create anxiety and feelings of despair knowing they're unable to do anything to help. Again, I can't believe this is happening. I feel nauseous and shaky.

I breathe in deeply, and try to slow everything down. A little voice enters my thoughts, 'Give up? You don't give up.' It's the voice of the corporal who had trained me.

Something strong surges inside of me, pushing at me to turn a switch in my mind. I'd experienced this once before, during my training. It had happened at the point where I'd become exhausted from physically and mentally exerting myself so far and so hard and for so long. The demands made had been unrelenting, and when I'd reached what I thought was the end, we'd had to go even further. At the time there was always something there to make me do it. I'd had to cast doubt aside, and had had to believe I could and would keep going.

Now I'm in that situation once again. We need to push beyond the boundaries of what seems possible. We have to grit our teeth and keep going.

"Jeremy, I have a really strong feeling that if we can just keep going, we'll be rescued. They will get to us. I just know it. They will."

"We'll pull through," Jeremy insists. "We'll keep each other warm, and I'll patch up the drafty holes with more ice. We'll be okay."

It's reassuring hearing Jeremy's voice. I'm not on my own. I snuggle closer to him. He hugs me against his chest. I feel his hand through his glove as he gently grips my arm. It's comforting and I'm overcome by a strong urge to drift off to sleep.

He continues. "It won't be easy, but I know we can do one more night."

"Okay," I whisper.

It's tempting to sink back. Perhaps if I just relax a bit more, the shivering will go away. Quickly I open my eyes and sit up straight. Now is not the time to relax.

"I'll text, 'Thanx Avery, not yet.'"

Over the wind we hear the 'beep, beep' sound and the 'message sent' sign comes up.

A couple of minutes pass and we receive a new message from Avery. I read it to Jeremy. 'I am moving heaven and earth to get you out.'

"Right, let's move our positions and do some more foot rubbing. We can't let him down."

It's as though it's not my voice speaking. It's someone more authoritative and in control. My body merely obeys the commands, too exhausted to protest.

We wriggle around, then set about banging our feet and hands to shake away the frostbite. My feet are swollen and bruised, and when the life oozes back into them they feel battered and sore. Each time the circulation takes longer to return. But I know we have to keep going.

10 P.M.

Prolonged exertion has exhausted our body's reserves until it becomes difficult for me to keep a grip on the shelter. My fingers are numb, like fat sausages that won't respond. They start to uncurl. I know if I accept what's happening to my body, the battle will be lost. It's important to shut out negative thoughts. Positive visualisation is something climbers use in competitions, or when they're about to tackle an impossible-looking route. By working through the process in your mind, by imagining yourself succeeding, you're able to programme your mind into being successful. By imagining your muscles moving efficiently, you're able to encode them to do so. This is called programming your engrams – the muscle's ability to remember how to operate or move. It is said even the thought process themselves can build muscle memory within your muscle fibres.

I try to think about these engrams as I keep a grip on the shelter. The fear of a horrible icy death is keeping me going. Eventually I'm just too weak to hold on any more, and Jeremy presses my clenched fist between his leg and the surrounding rock to prevent my fingers from opening.

I don't think we'll receive any more messages, and am about to switch off the phone. 'Rega' flashes up, and I read it out.

'Keep going, weather improves. We are doing everything we can. We will try tomorrow. Geri.'

The weather isn't improving where we are, but this gives us hope. The light of my torch flashes across Jeremy's face. He is dozing off. I shake him. "Jeremy, wake up." He opens his eyes and closes them again. I pinch his arm. "Jeremy you must stay awake."

"Okay, okay, I'm awake," he mutters. It had been Jeremy who'd set up the abseils, who'd jumared back up the ropes, who'd taken the lead on our escape from the electric storm to this ledge. Now it's my turn to take over. I decide to let him rest for ten minutes. I look at my watch and switch off my torch. I know this is dangerous, as I now have to stay awake or we'll both perish.

I think back to my training in the army, trying to remember some of the things I'd written in my diary. I'd memorised a few of these lines, so that when I was confronted by a similar situation during training I could say the words over and over in my head, like a mantra, to keep me going.

It's been a few years since I've had to recall the words: 'This game is more in the mind than in the body. The mind always shuts down before the body. It tells you, you cannot go on. It creates failure before failure exists, and allows despair to breed in place of hope. That only happens if you let it. We have trained our minds to change a failing situation into success; not to surrender, and to strive for excellence in everything we do. We have proved success to ourselves, like the many that walked before us.'

I repeat these words to myself in the dark. I imagine myself running up hills, carrying a heavy army backpack, my limbs feeling weak. In my mind I see myself struggling, and yet managing to wade through another river, and another, until I reach the end of the course. I remember the training sessions called 'beastings', how they hurt, and how they felt as if they would never end.

Our lack of sleep, excruciating physical and mental fatigue, and fear of a never-ending situation, is just like a long 'beasting' session. The only difference is, of course, that in my army training I could have given up at any time and it would not have cost me my life. Here if we give up, we will never see our families and friends again.

I try to list reasons why we can and need to keep going. It is difficult. My brain doesn't want to focus and I keep forgetting what I've just thought. I try to think of five good reasons – to allocate one to each finger. I determine, when I've memorised these, that I'll tell them to Jeremy. I'm battling to remember, and need his help. I shine my torchbeam on his face.

"Jeremy, we need to change positions, and then we must do our list."

He doesn't say much, but dutifully shifts. Carefully and slowly we move over and around each other without tearing the sheet. Eventually we settle facing each other, our legs wrapped round one another. We tilt our head torches to the side so the beams don't shine directly into our eyes. The shelter is filled with light reflecting off the blue sheet and the ice that has formed inside the fabric.

Jeremy pulls off his gloves and takes my foot in his hands. Slowly he undoes the fastenings and pulls off my shoe. Usually I'd not be keen for a man I liked to see me, or my swollen feet, in this state. I watch as he carefully lifts my foot in his hand and brings it towards his mouth. He blows onto my icy white toes. Then he rubs each toe, and when he finishes he gently places my foot back in the shoe, and starts on the other.

He doesn't say anything. I'm embarrassed, as we really haven't experienced this sort of intimacy before. Slowly I reach across and fumble with his shoelaces. His feet are white and hairy, but I don't mind. There's something about the process that goes beyond the ugliness of our situation, and it's strangely beautiful in a way too difficult to describe. A small fire has kindled inside me and, however cold my body is, the fire is growing stronger.

"Um, Jeremy ..." I lean forward, pulling his head closer, whispering into his ear. "If I had to be on this ledge with anyone, I would have wanted it to be you."

His hand curls round my shoulder, then reaches up and brushes the hair behind my ear. He leans towards me.

"Me too," he says, and kisses my cheek.

I'm excited, exhausted, cold, and hot at the same time. A sudden gust of wind howls around us and we grip the edges of the sheet again. Our moment of romance has been short, but that little fire inside me glows for a good while longer.

We start on our list of reasons to keep going. I'm shocked at how poor my concentration and memory have become, but together we manage to help each other remember.

Five reasons why we can survive:

1. The rescue team knows where we are. We will be rescued.
2. We are healthy and of above average fitness.
3. We have created a routine, and have stuck to our routine so far. Our routine works.
4. We have each other.
5. We still have a few peanuts!

The list could have looked quite different. There are at least six reasons why we might not survive:

1. We are suffering from hypothermia.
2. Our limbs are becoming frostbitten.
3. We have not slept for two days, and physically and mentally exerted ourselves for eighteen hours prior to arriving on the ledge.
4. We have not had anything to drink since Saturday afternoon. All our liquid is frozen, so we are very dehydrated.
5. We have not had a proper meal since Friday lunchtime, before our ascent to the hut.
6. The storm is showing no sign of abating and no one can get to us in these conditions.

We begin to run out of ideas to keep us awake and mentally alert. The urge to slump back and close our eyes intensifies after each task. Jeremy suggests we count the little squares making up the shelter's ripstop weave. Each square is roughly half a centimetre wide, and it would have been difficult enough for me to try counting them even after a week of good sleep and healthy living. But doing it now will certainly stop us from thinking about our gloomy prospects, or from falling sleep. We start counting. We work out how many squares there are in one square metre of fabric, in ten metres, in a kilometre! After a while I feel as if the counting is a dream, and I'm dreaming I'm trying to stay awake. I have to move, and we need to do more foot rubbing.

11 P.M.

We have only a couple of peanuts left. Our spirits are pretty low. It's taking longer and longer to warm up our feet. The energy it takes to bang life back into them is weakening us further. We know there's no chance of our surviving another day like this. We've run out of banter. It's a couple of hours from our official 'phone time', but we can't hold out any longer. I'm afraid to switch it on, though, in case nothing comes up.

There is a message from Avery:

'We are still working for you. They will make an attempt at dawn.'

I want to cry, but my tear ducts are dry. I can't give up now. Dawn is only eight hours away. Eight hours – a lifetime. I can't imagine myself being able to stay awake even two hours more. Eight hours is four times as much. We've come so far, but things are now just becoming impossible.

1 A.M.

The wind's long, slow moaning continues to funnel up from the crevasses, gathering momentum and volume on its course. It explodes in a cacophony of sound. The human mind can adapt to situations very quickly. It's no longer a new experience. It's our life. We have adapted to a miserable existence and become familiar with it. We're now beyond fear, and our life flickers like a slowly fading candle.

Jeremy keeps slumping over, and it's becoming more difficult to rouse him. I feel his grip loosen round my waist as he drifts between the present and a more pleasant place. I've told him just about every motivational story I know. Only one remains. I've kept it as a last resort. Now, at 1 a.m. in the morning, it seems like the right time.

"Ten years ago I was rock climbing in New Hampshire, North America. My friend and I set up camp in a remote forest. Around midnight, we were woken by the thud of something pouncing on the tent. My immediate reaction was to yell as loudly as possible. We were both awake, alert and listening in the dark. A breeze rustled through the canopy of leaves, and somewhere above a twig snapped. Nothing happened for a few long minutes. I was about to snuggle back into my sleeping bag when something again leapt on the tent. We both hollered.

"The beast sprang off and then charged the tent again, ripping the nylon with its claws. In desperation my friend stabbed at it through the fabric with a penknife. I scrambled in the darkness to find my hiking boots, and grabbed the small gas cooker as a weapon. We could hear a sickly yelping, 'Oww! Oww!' We only had one head torch with us in the tent, which wasn't much help in the darkness.

"Soon we were in battle. I caught a glimpse of the beast as it lunged my way. It appeared to be a large coyote, but I couldn't be sure. I yelled and waved the cooker at it. It jumped up at me, and I ducked out of the way. Although we really couldn't see what it was we could hear the patter of its paws on the dry leaves as it circled us.

"'Quick, it's to your left!' I shouted as I caught a glimpse of fur bounding through the air. We yelled and waved our penknife and cooker at the animal to ward off the attack. As quickly as it came, it was gone, and again we were left with the pitter-patter of the stalking beast somewhere out of sight. The next time it lunged at my arm, and I leapt sideways and swung the cooker forcefully. We jumped, darted and lunged, and then waited. 'Oww! Oww' It was taunting us from somewhere just out of sight.

Then a pair of wild eyes glistened red in the torchlight and the beast was at my climbing partner's throat. 'Arghhh!' I shouted and tried to hit the furry body. We stood shivering with adrenaline, listening for the rustle of leaves or a snapping twig on the ground. We scanned the immediate foliage with the torch's weak beam. It was unable to penetrate more than a few metres. We spent almost an hour fighting off our attacker with just the cooker and a penknife, before it disappeared.

We listened, breathing as softly as we could, and waited. About fifteen minutes passed and we decided to light a fire just in case the wild one returned."

Jeremy's breathing is heavy. I shake his arm and he opens his eyes, "I'm listening. What happened next?"

I continue.

"I crouched down and scraped the earth away with my hands. I blew the smoke and stoked it with a twig. It sparkled and a little orange light flickered. More dry twigs were added and the little flame gobbled these too. Finally it roared and a large flame leaped high.

"We took it in turns to collect wood to keep the fire going, and when it was my turn my nerves tingled with each step away from our fire. I collected some large branches and dragged them back. We swapped the head torch, dragging back our find, until we had satisfied ourselves we had enough fuel to keep the flame going all night. I cast a look back, and there was our tent, ripped from a savage attack, and only partially erect.

"By now we had salvaged our sleeping bags from the wrecked tent, and placed them around the fire. We laid out our most lethal pieces of metal climbing equipment, and sharpened some of the sticks to create 'spears'. We took turns to be 'on guard'.

"It wasn't long before the animal returned, and lunged at my friend's ankle with its teeth. Within seconds we were again in battle, swinging the climbing equipment like a cat o' nine tails, and jabbing through the flames with our wooden spears. For the next couple of hours we stood back to back, one of us throwing more wood on the now roaring fire, and the other fending off the savage attacker. It had no fear of the fire, and repeatedly leapt through the flames. In a final crazed attack it pounced into the fire and bit into a burning ember. We couldn't believe our eyes as we watched the ember bounding off through the dark.

"Quickly I loosened the coils on our climbing rope and knotted a carabiner to one end. I tossed the carabiner in the air so that it flipped over a high branch. Amazingly the rope slithered over the branch behind it, and tumbled in a loop to the leafy floor below. I tied a knot where the two ropes met and hauled myself up the lines, climbing arm over arm to reach the branch. I tied myself in the tree with a couple of slings, and then hauled up the remains of our supplies. Finally I knotted the rope to form notches to climb up, and my friend joined me on the branch opposite.

"We remained there till dawn, hoping the beast would not return, and prove to be an excellent tree climber as well.

"The dawn chorus started, oblivious to our harrowing experience, and soon the sky had changed from pitch black to a dusty grey. Reluctantly we slithered down the ropes to prepare for our escape on foot. It wasn't long before I heard voices and saw a young couple striding down the path with ropes on their back. It seemed wise to warn them, and now slightly dazed from our extraordinary experience and lack of sleep, I stumbled into the path.

"My clothes were singed, my hair was wild and tangled, and my eyes were still wide with fright. Quickly I exchanged greetings and began to recount our experience. The couple looked startled. Then the man became quite frightened and asked me to describe the wild animal. I started relating its size, the colour of its fur, its eyes, its sharp teeth, when he interrupted and pointed behind me, trembling.

"'It's not like that one behind you?' he stammered. I swung round, and saw the beast bounding down the path towards me. It leapt at me, and I screamed loudly and punched at it. My friend grabbed a nearby log, and as it leapt towards him he swiped at the beast and hit it with a terrific blow. It fell dazed to the ground, and quickly my friend brought the log down onto the creature with several hard blows, until its skull cracked, and a mixture of blood and grey matter splattered across the log and onto his clothing.

"The climbers stood horrified, speechless, glued to the ground. Soon a few other people arrived, and along with them a vet, who associated the peculiar behaviour of the creature – now identified as a common fox – as a symptom of rabies. The rest of our vacation was spent largely in hospital clinics, waiting to receive post-exposure rabies injections, or recovering from the symptoms the injections produced."

2 A.M.

The hours trudge by. The gale continues. There appears to be no respite.
By 2 a.m. we reach breaking point. I'm shaking with cold, virtually
unable and unwilling to move even a fraction. Things are sliding out of
control, and our end is hastening to meet us. The battle is over.

I resign myself to the fact that no matter how hard I try, or believe,
or 'keep going', I need to acknowledge the truth of how close we are to
the end.

There is only one thing left for us to do, and for just a moment I
hesitate before mentioning it to Jeremy. This is the sort of thing I
normally keep to myself, a long way from a first date. But then this hasn't
been an ordinary date. In a few days together we've shared some deep
emotions and singularly unusual experiences. We feel as if we've known
each other for years.

"Jeremy, I think we should pray."

"Okay." He is awake and sitting up.

"Shall I start?" I whisper.

"Yes, that would be good." He squeezes my arm.

I put my hands together. "Dear God ..." How strange this feels, but I
continue anyway. "Dear God, please spare our lives. Dear God, please
look after us until they come. Keep us going. Please be with the rescue
team as they try to get to us, and we pray for our families, and for Avery."

It's really weird. As I start praying for Avery and the rescuers, I begin
to imagine things from their perspective. They must be so worried, and
tired. It must be a horrible nightmare for them.

"Please be with Avery, and help him sleep. He must be so worried, and
he has been such a good friend. Please give the rescuers the strength
they need, and God give us courage to hold out till then. Please, God, we
ask you take this storm away so they can get to us safely. Amen."

I don't want to go on too long, and am pleased when I hear another
"Amen" from Jeremy.

Afterwards we feel a tiny bit better. Jeremy suggests another position
swap, and that we open the empty peanut packet and lick the plastic.
For a short while I've been sitting on the outside, and have been shaking

from the cold draughts piercing the shelter into my back. Once we swap positions I settle back between Jeremy's legs, and am thankful for it. Without him I would not have survived this long. Sharing and working together has been integral to our survival.

3.30 A.M.

We are awake and rubbing feet and hands again. It takes me about twenty minutes of furious tapping and massaging before the blood seeps back into each finger and toe. When I've just about finished one, the other foot is cold again, and I have to start all over. My eyes feel glassy and I'm shaking and nauseous.

I sit back for a few minutes and listen to the wind howling up from way below, growing louder. Again we hold on tight as it tries to rip our shelter away. While we're doing this we can't warm our feet.

Perhaps my mind is becoming fuzzy, but it seems the intervals between each gust – and our having to hold on tight – are growing longer. It reminds me of being in the Namib Dessert with my parents, and thinking we can hear the sound of a vehicle across the desert. We didn't know if our minds were playing tricks on us, and refused to believe it until the vehicle was close by and there was no denying the sound. I spend a good few minutes listening and waiting before opening my mouth.

"Jeremy, I think the storm is dying down a bit. Am I dreaming?"

I can't get the words out properly. We both stop our foot beating, keeping as quiet as we can, pricking our ears to the sounds to which we've grown so accustomed. After what seems an age, Jeremy replies.

"The storm is not so strong. They will try in the morning."

I say something in reply, but the words came out the wrong way round, and I can't sort them out in my head. Not long till daylight, I think, yet I can't bear to count the hours. Instead of being able to hold out for a few hours till our next 'reward', I'm looking at my watch every few minutes, willing away minutes as the hand moves round. I'm desperate for something to drink. I reach under the shelter and scrape at the snow outside, dragging back a fistful. I stuff it in my mouth and, for a split second, hope it hasn't been urinated on. I don't care. I need to get something into my aching stomach.

In basic psychology, students study Maslow's Hierarchy of Needs. It identifies a hierarchy of sophistication and order of needs. At the apex of the pyramid are sophisticated desires such as those for leisure and love. Further down are more basic needs, until right at the bottom are the needs for food and shelter.

By this definition we'd started pretty high up the hierarchy – going on a date and participating voluntarily in a sporting activity. When things started to go wrong, though, we were very quickly starved of the basic requirements, and slowly our minds and bodies changed, too. Initially, we were able to communicate effectively and to work together to solve problems.

As we became more tired, cold, hungry, and thirsty, and as our chance for rescue receded, we began to sink rapidly down the hierarchy. We stopped caring about pleasantries, and after a while it became more difficult to control our thoughts and consider detailed concepts.

It is becoming harder to continue thinking about each other. By 4 a.m. I can't string simple sentences together. Eventually, I can't physically care for Jeremy, and my efforts are expended solely on my own survival. Just exchanging a few simple words becomes a big effort, and our communication is limited to incomprehensible grunts and mumbles.

4.30 A.M.

Trying to do things to a time frame is beyond me. In my own battle to survive I'm only half aware of Jeremy's presence. The selfishness of my actions contradicts everything we've built upon. To get this far we've relied on combining our knowledge, skills, and experience, yet now I'm reluctant even to shift my body to allow Jeremy some extra warmth. He's been fundamental to my survival, and has helped on so many levels. I rummage in my pockets for sweet wrappers to lick, and find nothing, so I set about shaking my hands and rubbing them together. My mouth utters strange sounds, a kind of moan, and I don't care if Jeremy hears or not. I press my arms into my sides and shiver. I rock back and forth trying to warm myself. Nothing works.

6.30 A.M.

I'm drifting between the next world and the one I'm fighting to remain part of. Finally the sky lightens, breaking the monotony of the night. The wind has calmed. We can wait no longer. Jeremy hands me the phone. In a daze I press the number. The battery flickers on two bars, then drops to one. I'm certain this will be the last communication. The number rings. We hold our breath.

"Hello."

"Hello, this is Rachel. We are okay."

It's strange to hear my voice. Again, it's not my voice, but someone else's sounding controlled and unemotional.

"Rachel! You are okay?" The man sounds surprised and happy. It's as if they really were not expecting us to be conscious by this stage.

"Yes, we're fine. The weather is clear, and no wind."

"Yes. We plan to come for you just after seven. You are okay?"

"We are fine. Very little battery in the phone."

"Okay. Switch it on when you hear us coming. We will be there after seven."

"Okay. Goodbye."

I hand the phone to Jeremy. Finally, it seems, the nightmare is about to end.

13 Rescue

Chance only favours the prepared mind.
Louis Pasteur

Jeremy

'Wop, wop, wop.' At 7 a.m. we heard the sound of the helicopter ascending from the valley below. It took some minutes to rise up the sharp, snowy ridge, presumably taking care in the thinner air and possibly taking into consideration air turbulence.

Rachel stayed wrapped beneath the shelter. She was now very cold and shivering uncontrollably. I was concerned that in her current state she could easily slide into unconsciousness, and if they aborted the rescue it would be too much for her. When she had held out for so long, it was the last thing we needed.

The Alouette looked like a giant yellow wasp as it flew past us. From my mountain rescue experience it looked as if the pilot was doing a dummy run. On its next pass someone would be lowered from the helicopter and would attempt a rescue.

I stayed outside the shelter to indicate our position, and made the international signal for 'help' with my arms. They waved at me, and I waved back. Then they turned and flew away, down across the glaciers and towards the valley. What could be the problem? I dared not say anything to unnerve Rachel, so I told her they would be back in a couple of minutes, and that this was normal procedure.

I was becoming very cold, but I didn't want to miss any signal or opportunity to assist the rescue team in getting to us. I counted each second as it passed. Some time later the Alouette returned with something attached to a long cable. I couldn't quite make out what it was. Perhaps there was another reason they had flown back. Perhaps they still could not get to us because of our inaccessible position, and this was a parcel of supplies. I stared intently at the lump hanging way below the helicopter. It must have been about eighty metres below the craft.

Slowly the helicopter came closer and closer. The 'package' became evident ... a man suspended on the cable. I had never seen such a long-line rescue, and suspected the rescuers were attempting something that may not have been done before. Again I didn't mention this to Rachel.

By now the clatter of blades was drowning out our voices, and I stepped back from the edge, behind the rock parapet. I shouted to Rachel, and tapped at her through the shelter. From being sluggish only a few minutes before, she sprang into action, trying to stuff the shelter into her rucksack and tugging on the zip that predictably jammed at just the wrong moment.

Meanwhile the man on the cable was manoeuvred onto our ledge by giving instructions through his lapel to the pilot above.

There was an incredible synergy between man and machine as the rescuer coordinated his instructions, until he was able to grab the edge of the parapet and climb over it onto the ledge. He released the cable from his harness.

I was still feeling apprehensive. The initial phase of the rescue mission had been executed safely, but we were only a third of the way through. Much could happen between now and us landing safely in the valley below. The Alouette flew away.

The rescuer stood between us and the edge and immediately examined our sit-harnesses. Other than a few basic instructions in a mixture of Swiss German and English, the rescuer used gestures to show us what he wanted us to do.

He checked the buckles and motioned to us to take off the ropes we had coiled and placed over our shoulders. Next he pointed at our chests. My heart sank as I realised he was expecting us to have been wearing chest harnesses. I vaguely remembered Rachel saying something about this after one of our communications with the rescue team. We had opened our rucksacks to get the slings out but, by that stage, our concentration was compromised and we had dropped one of the slings. It had quickly frozen into the ice beneath us.

The rescuer sprang into action, pulling some slings from his rucksack. He constructed a makeshift harness by knotting two slings together and passing it around my torso, dexterously tying the ends together despite wearing insulated mountaineering gloves. He reached into his bag to make another harness for Rachel, but all he could find was a single piece of nylon cord. He uttered further instructions through his mike to his colleagues in the air.

Even in the state she was in, Rachel knew exactly what to do. It was as if she had found new energy, and unzipped her bag to grab another sling.

'Wop, wop, wop.' The Alouette returned with a second rescuer who was deposited neatly behind us. The small ledge was becoming very crowded, and I hoped they wouldn't be sending any more people down on long lines. We now had a rescuer on either side of us.

I felt a tap on my shoulder, and turned away from helping Rachel, to the first rescuer.

He waved his index finger from side to side indicating I should stop what I was doing, and then he beckoned me towards him. He was now holding the end of the cable the other rescuer had just been lowered on.

When I was on the helicopter rescue team in South Africa, we had been taught that if the cable we were attached to became snagged, the pilot would be forced to flick a switch that would sever it, in order to save the aircraft and crew. This was a risk to which all mountain rescue workers consent. I summoned energy into my legs and shuffled towards him. My head was dizzy and my mind was foggy. It wouldn't be long now. I just needed to stay focused for a little while longer.

The rescuer attached me to the hook on the end of the cable. Simultaneously it went slack as the helicopter was hit by a downdraft and the cable began to slide into a crack on the parapet. "Don't twist and get stuck," I prayed. These would be the most dangerous few moments, as they tried to manoeuvre us off the tiny protrusion of rock. The rescue worker clipped into the same cable, and I realised I was leaving Rachel behind.

Rachel looked up as the other rescue worker tended to her. Her eyes were wide and glassy. I trusted him to look after her, and didn't want her to feel scared. I summoned up the strength to try and appear calm and confident, as if this was as normal as alighting from a train.

We stood together on the edge of the parapet. The cable went tight as the helicopter gained elevation, and I felt a sharp tug as we were plucked off the ledge, and made a giant swoop outwards, under the aircraft.

Some minutes later we were being lowered to the ground. A man came up and guided me into the Sciora Refuge. The last thing I saw before going inside was the helicopter heading up towards Rachel and her rescuer.

A short while later Rachel appeared at the door and we were reunited. Subsequently we learned this had indeed been the longest line rescue of its kind ever attempted in Europe.

It all happens fairly quickly. I watch numbly as Jeremy swoops from the ledge and disappears into the distance. It's as if I'm losing a limb. I watch intently as he becomes a small speck and then vanishes.

Meantime the second rescue worker asks me a few questions and sets about checking my harness and creating a chest attachment. He isn't the young, athletic man you might imagine. He has a lined face and white beard, and for a moment I think he must be someone's grandfather. In my semi-delirious state his voice sounds distant, and I imagine him in another context, at Christmas with his children and grandchildren. I wonder if they know what his work really entails. I feel thankful, but somewhat dislocated from what is going on.

The helicopter returns and drowns out any further communication. The journey looks rather frightening, but at this stage I'm not about to protest. The man holds me by my arms, attaches me with a sling, and suddenly we're lifted from the ledge. I cling onto him as we swing out.

We fly swiftly over the huge space where cliffs drop hundreds of metres below us. I glance back to the tiny ledge where we've spent all that time. It soon shrinks into the horizon of the mountain, and is no longer visible. We whizz high over the glaciers and hover above the Sciora Refuge. I can see another small red and white helicopter. It's the air ambulance – on standby to transfer us to hospital at St Moritz should it be necessary.

As we descend on the eighty metre-long cord beneath the helicopter, I'm not sure what to expect, and hold on tightly. Ever so gently we touch down. Although we've landed and I'm standing upright, I can't feel anything beneath me, and once we're unclipped it's difficult to move.

With some help from my rescuer, I shuffle around the side of the building and pull on the wooden door handle. It's warm and dark inside, and takes me a few seconds to adjust to the light. A doctor sits in the corner, examining Jeremy's feet. He beckons. I hobble towards him.

He motions for me to take off my shoes and sit alongside Jeremy on the wooden bench. Gently he lifts each foot and examines it, carefully prodding the small purple areas on my toes and around the backs of my heels. I can't feel very much. The tissue around the dark bits is white, but thankfully regains a pinkish hue when he presses on them. I don't need to be told about the purple bits. They are frostbitten, areas of flesh frozen and dead. Providing no infection sets in, they will eventually harden and separate, peeling off like thick scabs once the new tissue has formed beneath. There will probably be scarring and, undoubtedly, I will never regain full sensitivity or circulation in those areas. On any future ventures in cold places I will need to take special care. As he checks my feet and studies our hands, he raises his eyebrows and shakes his head. I'm a little worried, and too afraid to ask.

One of the team who has peered over my shoulder inquisitively during the examination, hands us both a hot drink. He breaks the silence.

"Iz not black? How you manage thees?"

Slowly I begin to understand. It isn't concern that's raised the doctor's eyebrows. It's surprise. They were expecting whole limbs of frostbite, not just a few patches here and there. We're unable to communicate in either Italian or German, so we demonstrate our foot- and hand-warming technique. There are nods all round.

"For long time?" the rescuer asks.

I show him on my watch, "Every hour, then later, when very cold, every twenty minutes ... for two days, no sleeping."

The man laughs. "I don't believe! Very good. Iz very good!"

There are more smiles and nods all round. They seem pretty taken aback we've survived as long as we have, and have managed to maintain our health with limited supplies in such a freak storm.

We gratefully accept the hot drinks and hand- and foot-warming pads to help with the return of circulation. It's a bit of a shock being back with people in a warm and civilised environment. We hear people speaking normally without having to shout against the noise of the gale. Part of me is still on the ledge, and I need time for my brain to catch up with my body.

Once we've been thoroughly checked over by the doctor, he suggests they fly us to hospital by helicopter, where they'll defrost us slowly in baths of warm water.

Although thoroughly exhausted and weak, we're reluctant to extend our ordeal with more helicopter flights and a stay in hospital. Costs are mounting. We decide, in spite of grave misgivings on the part of the doctor, to drive to the nearest hotel where we can rest and allow our bodies to recover. Our rescuers offer to fly us to our vehicle and to collect our backup rucksack en route.

14 Reality sinks in

In the mountains, worldly attachments are left behind,
and in the absence of material distractions,
we are opened up to spiritual thought.
We should be attempting to carry the spiritual experience
of the mountains with us everywhere.
JAMLING TENZING NORGAY

The helicopter drops us in a field near our car, and once we've sorted ourselves out, all the rescuers come over to shake our hands. I really have to bite back the tears.

As I shake each of their hands, I remember the desperation of being only metres out of reach a day earlier. I picture the tiny faces looking at us from the helicopter rolling about in the storm. We're sitting on the frozen ledge, clinging to the hope they could just extend an arm to reach out to us.

I hardly know these people. I can't even remember all their names, and yet I know as long as I live, their faces will remain in my memory. Geri and the team supported us through our dark and lonely time on the mountain, encouraging us when we were at the end of our tether. Were it not for the uplifting text messages and attempted rescues, I would probably have given up hope, and my body would be lying up on that icy ledge waiting to be recovered.

We say goodbye, and they walk back to the field. As we push the last rucksack into the vehicle I hear the familiar sound of the helicopter rotor blades. The craft rises above the pine trees and flies away.

Adrenaline still pumps through our bodies. Despite not sleeping for over fifty hours and although we are battered and sore, our minds are buzzing with all the things we need to do. We have urgent phone calls to make. What follows is bizarre, surreal.

Jeremy starts the engine and carefully negotiates the bumpy track that follows the steep-sided ravine of the Bondasca River down to the village of Bondo. We each polish off an entire packet of Italian biscuits within minutes.

I plug the phone into the car charger. A string of messages follow. Through some of his associates, Richard has made emergency calls to the British Foreign Office in Switzerland. They've been trying to contact us, phoning repeatedly with encouraging messages, and updating us on progress they were making. There is a message from a concerned Ruth, and the earlier message from our friend Steve Gorton, the one that tells us the weather report had changed.

We call Avery and Richard. They are relieved we're alive. Next we call Steve, and then Ruth.

After the phone calls we have one last task. The base for the rescue workers is at the airfield in St Moritz. En route we purchase a large bottle of whisky and a card.

It takes us a while to find the Rega office, but no matter how weary we feel, we're determined to express our gratitude in some small way.

We can't find anyone, so we post the whisky and card through the letterbox. It an inadequate gift in return for our lives, but sincerely given.

As we drive from the airfield, Avery rings. He's getting calls from journalists, not just in Britain, but internationally. The story of our survival has grabbed their attention, it having been the first 'text message rescue' where a woman climber contacted friends across the continent to request a rescue from a mountain face.

"You'll probably get them calling you."

We find a public phone in the centre of St Moritz, and pour change into the coin slot. Jeremy hands me the receiver.

"You first," he says.

I dial Mum's mobile. "Hi Mum. We're in Switzerland."

"In Switzerland! What's the weather like?"

I smile. I break the news gently.

Next I phone Dad at home. But a journalist has beaten me to it. Despite the shock of the unexpected news, Dad has handled their conversation with equanimity and humour, saying he was thankful for our rescue, and felt confident we would have made the best decisions to survive under the circumstances. Dads have a habit of surprising one. Were it me, I probably wouldn't have been as poised had I received a shock phone call like that, especially knowing how much fathers worry about their daughters.

Jeremy's parents take the news in their stride. We're both relieved. No sooner have we finished talking to our parents than a journalist from *The Telegraph* calls us on my mobile. He wants a full account.

I think for a moment. It's nearly 2 p.m., and we've been awake almost sixty hours. We're completely worn out. I want to tell the journalist where to get off. I take a deep breath and bite my tongue. The story will be written anyway. If I'm rude, he'll write a hearsay piece that will not be a reflection of the truth. I summon some patience.

As it happens, *The Telegraph* reporter is interested in our ordeal from my perspective, possibly because it's rare to find women who climb technical or challenging mountains without guides leading their ascent. He wants to know what food we had, how we managed to stay awake, what kept us going, and whether we thought we had met our end.

As soon as we end the call, another call comes through, and then another ...

American television reporters want to fly camera crews to St Moritz to film us. And a news reporter asks for live footage of the rescue – which surprises me a bit. She agrees it's a bit of a long shot, but worth asking after anyway.

On our way we turn off the main road and drive up to a small village looking out over the Piz Badile. We stare across the valleys at the mountain, now cloaked in a glistening veil of snow and ice. An elderly couple offer to take a photograph of us, and we ask them to get the mountain in the background. The man follows our gaze to the mountain, "Is beautiful. You know zis mountains?"

"Yes, yes, it is beautiful," I agree.

We say goodbye and climb back into our car.

Completely exhausted, we're pleased later to find a beautiful Italian guesthouse near the airport. It's heaven to be able to sleep in a proper bed and to enjoy a warm shower. The next morning, before heading to the airport, we enjoy freshly percolated coffee and warm brioches. I glance at the television and am surprised to see something on the Italian news about two climbers being safely rescued. Could they be talking of us?

The flight home is uneventful. We fall asleep in our seats until the plane touches down in England. We're too hungry to wait to get home, and buy a full English breakfast at the airport. My feet are swollen and painful and, as we exit the terminal building, I shuffle over to the news-stand, curious to see if our story has been reported.

I flick open the first paper expecting to see a small column somewhere near the back, and am shocked to find page four devoted to our adventure. Our story has made the front pages of just about every other newspaper, and they've even managed to source photographs of us, and have drawn artist's representations of us texting from our shelter.

The Times displays a particularly amusing montage of me imposed on a snowy alpine ridge, climbing in a gym outfit. The incongruity of the summer outfit in a high-altitude environment makes us giggle. Jeremy is thankful the journalists have not done the same with him.

Back in England, we realise our lives have changed. As we drive from the airport, more reporters and news channels call us, hoping for updates. The BBC requests an interview in our homes. The man on the other end of the phone is so polite and understanding, I just can't refuse. A couple of hours later we're trying to hide all the underwear drying on the radiators in Jeremy's communal lodgings.

Over the next few days we hardly have a moment to ourselves as we field interviews for media around the world. Acquaintances from years before send messages to wish us well. Women's magazines are fascinated by our story, and I'm showered with gifts of bath salts and foot creams to help soothe the frostbitten areas. Reality TV makeover programmes want to treat me to pedicures where they'll be able to obtain gruesome close-ups of my frostbitten toes.

We're really keen to meet up with our friends, especially Richard and Avery. Richard can't stop smiling when he sees me. Being a medical student, he is fascinated to see the effects of frostbite first hand.

The *Sun* organises a special meeting for us to reunite with Avery at his photography studio in London. The photographer snaps a photo of me planting a kiss on Avery's cheek after I've raced to greet him, followed by one of Jeremy giving him a warm handshake and a hug.

"Oh man, it's good to see ya!" Avery keeps saying.

I feel lucky to have friends who care so much. At the end of one of the interviews, the reporter gives me her card saying if we have any further news I should give her a call. I think she imagines Jeremy and I might get married, or something.

I thank her, letting her know she will definitely hear from me if we have any more 'exclusive' news.

Over the days that follow the reality of our experience sinks in. Although I know the 'romance' of our survival on the mountain is not something to become carried away by, I miss Jeremy terribly when we're apart. We phone each other regularly, but ultimately we both have separate lives to lead.

At this point my life is full. I'm preparing for an expedition to Tibet in two weeks, and am getting my small climbing business, Kelsey Adventures, back on track. I'd been concerned our rescue would be bad news for my business, thinking people might view me as a risk taker. I couldn't have been more wrong. Suddenly everyone wants to join my climbing expeditions, and companies are booking me as a keynote speaker for conferences and evening events. We're also filming the final scenes for a television programme I'd been invited onto in the summer. Other opportunities have also cropped up.

It would have been the ideal time to throw myself headlong into work. Yet I keep thinking of Jeremy, wondering if he might also be thinking of me. Part of my life is empty, empty in a way it hadn't been before.

15 A perfect ending

Every new beginning comes from some other beginning's end.
SENECA

My expedition to Tibet is to help paraplegic explorer Glenn Shaw succeed in his goal of reaching Everest Base Camp in his wheelchair.

Each morning I anxiously pull my bedclothes away to study my feet, hoping their condition hasn't worsened overnight. After three or four days the swelling subsides, leaving discoloured bruising, which hurts when I try, rather optimistically, to squeeze into my climbing shoes. Of greater concern are the areas that don't hurt. A few of my toes have turned glassy white and have developed dark, purple-black patches where the cells have died. They hang like little dead marbles from my feet. Further discolouration appears around the back of my heels. I feel no pain, heat, cold or tickling, and I fear it might be spreading further, harbouring the possibility of amputation.

When Jeremy and I meet again we swap notes on our injuries. He's lost sensation in his right thumb and forefinger, and in part of his bottom, although these areas have not turned black. Overall his circulation has fared better than mine.

In the past surgeons amputated blackened areas to prevent gangrene. In the past I'd have been left with only five toes.

Jeremy and I meet with an old climbing friend – a surgeon, He checks our frostbite, and declares that as long as we maintain good care of the various areas, we'll probably be fine.

Before setting off for Tibet, I also seek advice from a climbing acquaintance who'd lost most of his fingers after summiting a series of technical Himalayan peaks. His advice is simple: If I want to keep my toes,

I should not let them get cold. Given the nature of my next expedition, where temperatures at night can plummet to −30 ºC, it will be difficult to guarantee this.

I consider whether it's wise to continue. I think about Glenn, about how much this means to him. Glenn has Brittle Bone Disease, which means he has to take great care not to fall or knock himself in case he breaks a bone. He has trained hard to be fit and healthy, and has gone to great lengths with the groundwork to ensure the expedition takes place. Then there are the others. The expedition co-leader, Neil, who's put so much preparation into our team mentally and physically. Ruth has raised thousands in sponsorship from Richard Branson's Virgin Active, Virgin Mobile and Canada Life, to cover costs and raise funds for the Whizz-Kidz charity for wheelchair-bound children. In choosing to support us, all these people have acknowledged the efforts we're making, and I'm not about to let anyone down. The entire team has dedicated time and energy, and each member is needed to make it a success.

I go through my boxes of extreme weather mountaineering equipment, searching out my warmest thermally-insulated boots, socks, and thermal boot liners that can be worn inside my sleeping bag at night.

The journey is to start in Nepal, from where we will fly to Lhasa in Tibet, then work our way east, cross-country to Everest Base Camp. A while back Neil had suggested I invite Jeremy on the expedition. At the time I was concerned about not having spent much time with Jeremy – that it might seem a bit forward. Now I wish I'd offered him the opportunity. A month seems an awfully long time to be away, and while I don't admit it openly, I've grown very fond of him. I hope in the meantime he won't just forget about me.

For a week our journey follows the rising sun, negotiating the high, snow-covered passes on unmade roads across the Tibetan plateau. Our destination is Rombuk. At an altitude of more than five thousand metres, it's the highest monastery in the world, and is close to Base Camp.

With our assistance, Glen has elected to push himself up the twelve kilometre ascent from Rombuk to Everest Base Camp. The journey is arduous. Thick snow covers the route. The wheelchair skids backwards whenever we slip on the icy ground or release any forward force. Over one hundred kilometre an hour gusts have us huddled in our tracks, masking our faces to protect them from the blizzard. My head is pounding from the altitude. Blood trickles from my nose, marking the snow and staining my balaclava.

That night I become very ill. I have a severe headache and am vomiting almost continuously. Our expedition doctor, Kim, is summoned. He immediately decides we must evacuate to a lower altitude. Accompanied by the chief Sherpa, Rinsin, and my climbing companion, Ruth, we travel through the snowy night down to Rombuk. Although some kilometres away, Rombuk is only a few hundred metres lower than where we've been.

During the night Kim works hard, administering drugs and checking the intravenous canular he's inserted is flowing correctly. The drugs take effect quickly and by dawn I feel much better – well enough to participate in the final push. Indeed, a couple of days later we heave Glenn in his wheelchair right up onto Mallory and Irvin's memorial cairn which acknowledges their very brave first attempt to summit Everest. We believe we've set a new world altitude record for a person in a wheelchair. The joy on Glenn's face is a picture that will live with me forever.

With careful monitoring I've kept my feet warm, and so I manage to complete the expedition with all ten toes intact. When we've had satellite phone reception, I've spoken to Jeremy. I miss him terribly, but don't know whether he feels the same about me. Each time we speak, I savour Jeremy's words for hours afterwards. I wonder if he might be doing the same, then am angry for being so sentimental. It's highly unlikely he'll even be giving our brief conversations a second thought. After all, he's so busy, climbing, working and doing a million and one other things. I decide it would be best not to think about him. Then, toward the end of the expedition, Jeremy asks whether, on my return, I have any immediate plans. He suggests we meet at the airport. I can't help but feel excited.

JEREMY

I knew how I felt about Rachel, but wasn't sure Rachel's feelings for me were the same. No man wants to feel rejected. I had to talk things through, and so drove down to Portchester to visit my aunt who had been a dependable ally for many years.

Over supper we had a good chat, and she was very encouraging. That night I stayed up late, thought things through, and made my decision. I have never been one to hang around once I know what I want. Before I left, my aunt gave me a family heirloom, and wished me luck. It was the Order of the Garter brooch my grandfather, an army captain, had given to Grandma during the war. She had worn it every day of her life from then on.

I decided that, if everything went to plan, the occasion I was plotting would be one we would remember. It seemed fitting to take Rachel back to the Piz Badile as a surprise.

Of course I was worried she might never want to see me or that mountain again, but I went with my instincts.

First I needed to check Rachel hadn't made other arrangements for her first weekend back in the UK, and then ensure she packed appropriate clothing. Our brief conversations via satellite link-up were to the point. Rachel believed I was planning to meet her at the airport, and we would then spend the weekend locally, just catching up. My real idea was to meet her at the airport, drop her at home, give her a few hours to repack some clothes, and then whisk her off to Switzerland, to go walking in the foothills.

As the plane touched down at Heathrow I'm sick with anticipation, hoping Jeremy will be there. What if he has changed his mind at the last minute, and doesn't want to see me after all? Passport control takes forever. Then my luggage does a disappearing act. An announcement explains the aeroplane was not loaded at Kathmandu, and that it may follow us on another flight due to arrive the following day.

Finally we emerge through the glass doors. I search the sea of waiting faces behind the barriers in the arrival lounge. There he is, right at the end, with a large bunch of yellow roses and a box of chocolates.

It's as if time has rolled back and, for a moment, I forget about everything except seeing him again. I can hide my feelings no longer and race over and hug him. Not only has Jeremy brought me flowers and chocolates, but he has another surprise. He waits until our team have said their goodbyes, then he hands me a card. Inside are two air tickets to Switzerland. We're to fly out that same day. I've never been treated like this before, and am bowled over – and hugely excited.

JEREMY

I arrived at the airport in good time. Everything went according to plan, until Rachel had to collect her luggage. Breezily she informed me of the mishap with the loading of the aircraft. I hadn't considered this. Her rucksack contained most of the warm winter clothing she'd need for our weekend away. But I felt I probably had sufficient for us both. Rachel, seemingly overwhelmed by the unexpected trip, didn't protest at my suggestion she borrow my spare thermals.

I'm pretty tired, but the excitement soon revives me. Some of my girlfriends have been whisked off on weekends away, but it has never happened to me. I feel rather special.

Over the next few hours my head spins as I collect myself after the long intercontinental flight, and adjust to the surprise of preparing for a romantic weekend. As we set off, Jeremy mentions we'll be revisiting the Piz Badile region to spend the weekend relaxing and walking in the mountains. I'm a little surprised at his choice, but am curious to see the mountain again and especially pleased to be able to share it with him.

Having travelled half way round the world since, it's strange driving again up the same narrow track to the Piz Badile. We park in a lay-by further down the hill. Snow covers the lane and I prod my walking sticks into the soft covering. We set off past the road cutting where we'd left our car before. I gaze across to the field from where we'd disembarked from the helicopter. It's also draped in white, a different world from the verdant undergrowth and thickly-scented autumnal leaves of October. Our final conversation with our rescuers, joking as they had been in their strong

Swiss accents as we'd shaken hands, echoes in my mind. We'd been so thankful to have our lives back that, despite our exhaustion, the colours had seemed so vibrant, and everything had teemed with life and energy.

We step off the track onto the path leading to the hut. I feel strange and emotional, and am not really sure why Jeremy has brought me back here. Everything is quiet. No wind, no animals rustling in the undergrowth, just soft, silvery flakes falling onto the outstretched limbs of sleeping conifers.

The track winds its way up the steep incline. As the snow becomes deeper, each step takes a little more effort. An hour has passed and Jeremy has said nothing, just held my hand intermittently, and squeezed my fingers through my thick woollen gloves.

A small wooden sign indicating 'Piz Badile' leads off through the trees and over a wooden bridge. Snow lies thick and undisturbed. It has gathered in large columns on the wooden posts, and is decorating the railings with shimmering sparkles. I look down into the fast-flowing, icy waters of the Bondasca River. Boulders sleep under thick white blankets. The crunch of Jeremy's footsteps in the snow stops. In the middle of the bridge Jeremy has turned around.

JEREMY

I was nervous when we set off, but it was to be expected. All the seemingly impossible climbs in some of the world's most remote locations I'd set out on, pale in comparison to what will possibly be the biggest step of my life. I had hidden the gold brooch in a small pouch of my travel bag, and had tried not to think too much. I'd planned to walk up towards the Piz Badile and to propose to her en route. When she wasn't looking, I tucked the brooch in my jacket pocket and took a deep breath. It was difficult not to ask her straight away, or the alternative to just keep walking and not to ask at all. Finally I made my move.

I hear him say, "Rachel Kelsey". I stop. My head swims, my heart races. He continues, "Will you marry me?"

I'm completely bowled over. I hadn't expected this at all. My heart is pounding. "Yes," I say, immediately.

Here I am, in the place where less than a month before I'd nearly died, and now I'm getting engaged to the man I know I love.

We reach out and hug each other. Above us the mist swirls slowly, enhancing the dream-white landscape and engulfing us both in a moment we'll never forget. Nature responds. Soft confetti snow showers our heads and sticks to our hair.

Epilogue

Sadly, our friends Seba and Richard, whom we'd texted from the mountain are no longer alive. Seba died descending from the summit of Mount Kenya in 2005. At his memorial service, I was privileged to meet his family from Switzerland and Italy, a family he'd so often mentioned. He left behind his sister Carlotta and his step-siblings. Carlotta and I are still in touch and she is now married.

Tragically Richard died in a canoeing accident in Scotland, also in 2005. Phil and other close friends tried to save him but were unable to do so. Richard was completing his studies as a doctor, as well as writing a book about sleep, and a children's novel. I feel honoured to have been asked to speak at his memorial service, but am so deeply sad to have lost such a caring friend. He was awarded his medical degree posthumously. His parents have dedicated a beautiful area of conservation land in Scotland to him, and each year his friends gather for a walk there, to remember him.

Ruth and I remain firm friends. She is now taking a break from her city career, and travelling around the world helping out where her skills can be put to use.

Tim was married in South Africa in 2007.

Avery is also married now, to a lovely woman who complements his zany, mid-west personality. He continues to work hard and successfully as a photojournalist, and they are about to set up home in New York.

Every now and then I e-mail the rescue workers who airlifted us from the mountain, updating them with our news and photos. We hope to meet up some time in the future ... just not in a helicopter.

Glossary

Aid climbing: Using climbing equipment in cracks and rock features and levering up on it. Aid climbing is different from free climbing where equipment is used as a backup should the climber fall.

Alpinism: Advanced, technical climbing which relies on skill, fitness, and speed. First practised in the European Alps.

Anchors: Climbing equipment fixed to a rock face so climbers can attach themselves at a belay stance.

Arête: A sharp-edged protrusion of rock, often like the vertices of a polygon, where two rock faces intersect.

Belay: To hold the ropes and catch the lead climber should they fall.

Belay device: Used to grip the belay rope.

Belay station: The point at which climbers stop to change over leads on a climb. Normally fifty metres apart (the length of a standard climbing rope).

Benighted: Colloquialism in climbing describing a situation where climbers have moved too slowly, or where for some other reason they have been stranded on a climb or in a reasonably inaccessible place as darkness falls.

Bergschrund: A deep gully of varying width between a rock face and a glacier. Often sheer-sided.

Bivi (bivouac): To spend a night or nights in the mountains with minimal provisions. Bivi equipment would include a waterproof cover for the sleeping bag, a sleeping bag, a small mat to lie on and a small stove in which to boil water or cook a meal.

Bivi bag: A waterproof cover made of breathable material and used to enclose a sleeping bag when camping without a tent. Can be zipped closed to create a cocoon.

Blank face: A rock face devoid of features.

Bulge: A large convex formation of rock that is often awkward to ascend.

Carabiner: Metal climbing equipment used to link ropes and pieces of climbing equipment together. It is a similar shape to a large link in a chain, with a simple spring gate which opens down one length, which may be locked in place with a screw sleeve over the gate.

Chimney: A long fissure or vertical crack that is wide enough to squeeze one's entire body into.

Chock: Also called 'nuts' or 'rocks', chocks are metal climbing devices which are wedged into cracks and secured to the climbing ropes to protect the lead climber in case of a fall.

Couloir: From the French word meaning 'corridor', a couloir is a seam or fissure of ice or snow in an otherwise solid mountain mass.

Crevasse: A steep-sided opening in a glacier.

Fissure: A crack or opening in a rock face or on a glacier.

Flake: To uncoil the rope in loops so that it runs easily through the belay device and does not become knotted.

Free climb: To climb using only the natural features of the rock, and not pulling up on safety equipment attached to the rock face. Safety equipment and ropes in this style of climbing are used only as a back-up to save the climber's life in the event of a fall. (See also 'Aid climbing'.)

Frostbite: A medical condition where cells stop receiving blood and freeze. Caused by prolonged overexposure to extreme cold.

Frostnip: The initial stage of frostbite – skin on the extremities turns white and becomes hard and glassy as it begins to freeze. It may begin to become discoloured.

Gear: Climbing equipment.

Gear placements: Cracks and fissures in a rock face into which climbing gear can be inserted.

Hoarfrost: Frozen stalactite type formations covering a surface, often extending horizontally, created by snow and wind.

Jumar (jumaring): A metal device used to ascend a rope, also known as an ascender. Jumaring is a method of ascending a rope.

Kloof: South African name for a steep-sided gorge.

Lead (leading, lead off): On an ascent, the person who goes ahead is the leader. The most experienced and able person generally leads. In competent climbing parties the lead alternates to give climbers a chance to lead different sections. If a person is guided up a climb, they will generally not take turns leading.

Multi-pitch: A long climb which is broken into smaller sections, or pitches, of up to fifty metres.

Norming: A term used in psychological profiling to indicate the stage at which a team settles prior to entering a phase of heightened productivity.

Overtrousers: Waterproof trousers with zips extending down the outside seams and worn over other garments.

Pegs: Metal or iron blades which are knocked into cracks in a rock face to protect or hold a climber in position. Similar to pitons.

Permafrost: The permanent ice on high mountains which holds together areas of fractured rock and loose soil. In recent years, with climate change, this ice has started to melt, resulting in large areas of rock fall, and physical change in alpine areas.

Piton: A blade-shaped iron wedge which is hammered into rock crevices to provide protection or create the base for a belay stance.

Protection: The climbing devices placed during a climb to prevent falls.

Prussic: A short length of cord tied in a loop. When wound around the abseil rope and clipped to the harness it tightens around the rope to keep the climber from sliding down the rope.

Rappel (rappelled): Derived from the French word meaning 'abseil'.

Sling: A long nylon strap stitched to form a continuous loop. A sling is normally one or two centimetres wide, and varies from ten centimetres to two and a half metres in length.

Smear (smeared): A footwork technique used to ascend a flat, vertical rock face.

Snout: The point at which a glacier ends.

Sport climbing: Climbing using fixed bolts that have been predrilled into the rock to clip the rope into for added safety.

Spire: A steeple-shaped protrusion of rock.

Stance: A small area, sometimes a small platform of rock, used as a belay station or place to swap over leads and sort out equipment, normally at fifty metre intervals. Where there is no ledge climbers hang from their harnesses. Often the stance has fixed equipment in which to clip.

Summit cairn: A beacon marker at the actual summit of a mountain, often comprising rocks piled on top of one another.

Verglas: A thin coating of ice overlaying a rock surface. Verglas is usually too thin to use crampons and ice axes on.

Sources

Maps:
Carte Nationale della Svizzera 1:25 000 Sciora, sheet no. 1296
Carte Nationale della Svizzera 1:25 000 Val Bregaglia, sheet no. 1276

Reference books:
Fergus Fleming, *Killing Dragons: The Conquest of the Alps* (Grove Press, 2002)
Lindsay Griffin, *Bernina and Bregaglia Selected Climbs* (The Alpine Club, 1995)
Chris Mellor, *Swiss Rock: Granite Bregaglia* (Void Publishing, 2000)
Robert Macfarlane, *Mountains of the Mind* (Granta, 2003)
Dictionary of Geography (Geddes and Grosset, 2001)

Website:
About Riccardo Cassin: http://www.cassin.it/uk/riccardo.htm

About Rachel

Rachel Kelsey Colenso was born in Pretoria, South Africa in 1969, and spent her youth in the Okavango Delta, Botswana, where her parents ran safaris. She was educated at the University of the Witwatersrand, and later completed a post-graduate degree in education through the University of Oxford.

In 1993 Rachel won the South African National Climbing Championships, and went on to train and serve with the British Special Forces. She has competed at international level in adventure races, featured in the programme *Superhuman*, and has appeared in advertising campaigns and as a sports model.

Rachel is honoured to be able to use her experience of extreme adventure to inspire audiences and provide insight into how teams and individuals perform in arduous, fightening or demanding situations.

As co-founder of Kelsey Adventures Ltd, Rachel has planned and lead expeditions for climbers and to promote ecological causes in remote locations across the world.

Rachel is married to Jeremy Colenso, and they have a baby daughter. They share their time between London and a conservation village near Cape Point, South Africa.

www.kelseycolenso.com
www.kelseyadventures.co.uk